AF604449
(a word to describe me)
(my name)

My progress chart

Find the letter to match your completed page. Track the letter and colour the picture.

a b c d

p o n m

q r s t

e
f
2
g
h
2
i
l
k
2
j
u
v
w
x
2
z
y

Help each animal find its home.

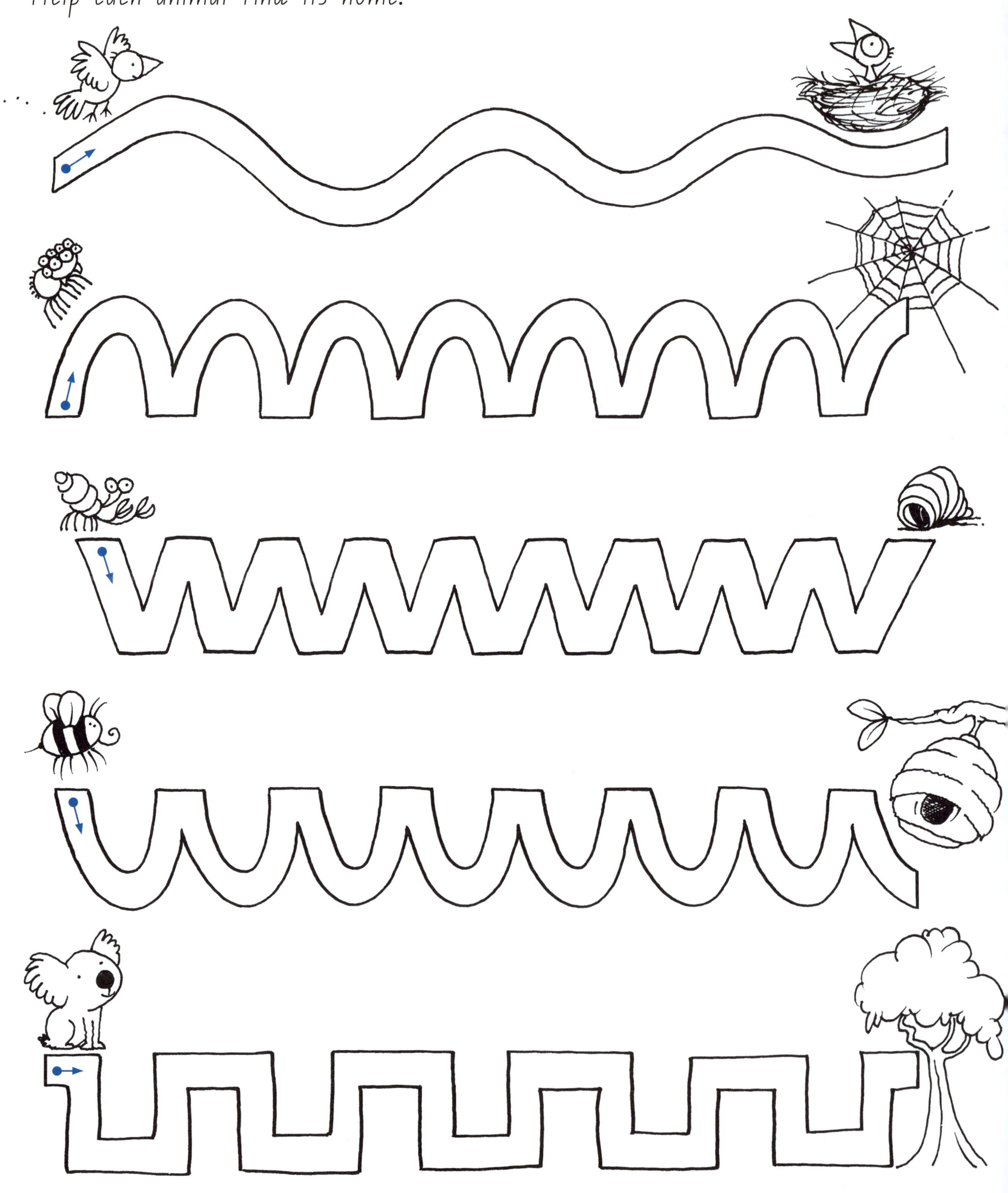

Handwriting: Tracking; left to right direction; fine motor control.

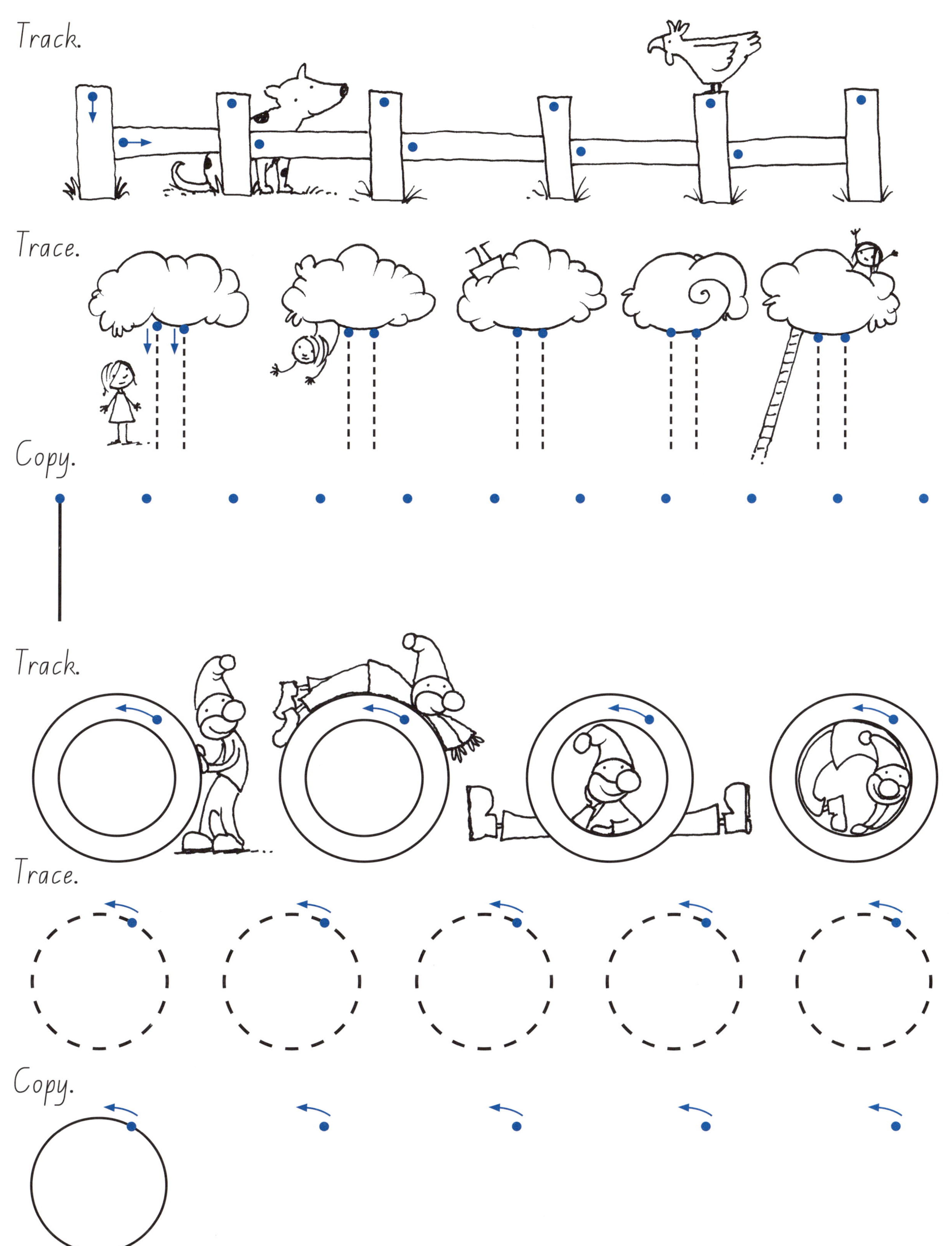

Handwriting: Patterning; left to right direction; anticlockwise direction; downstroke; forming parallel lines; fine motor control.

Trace.

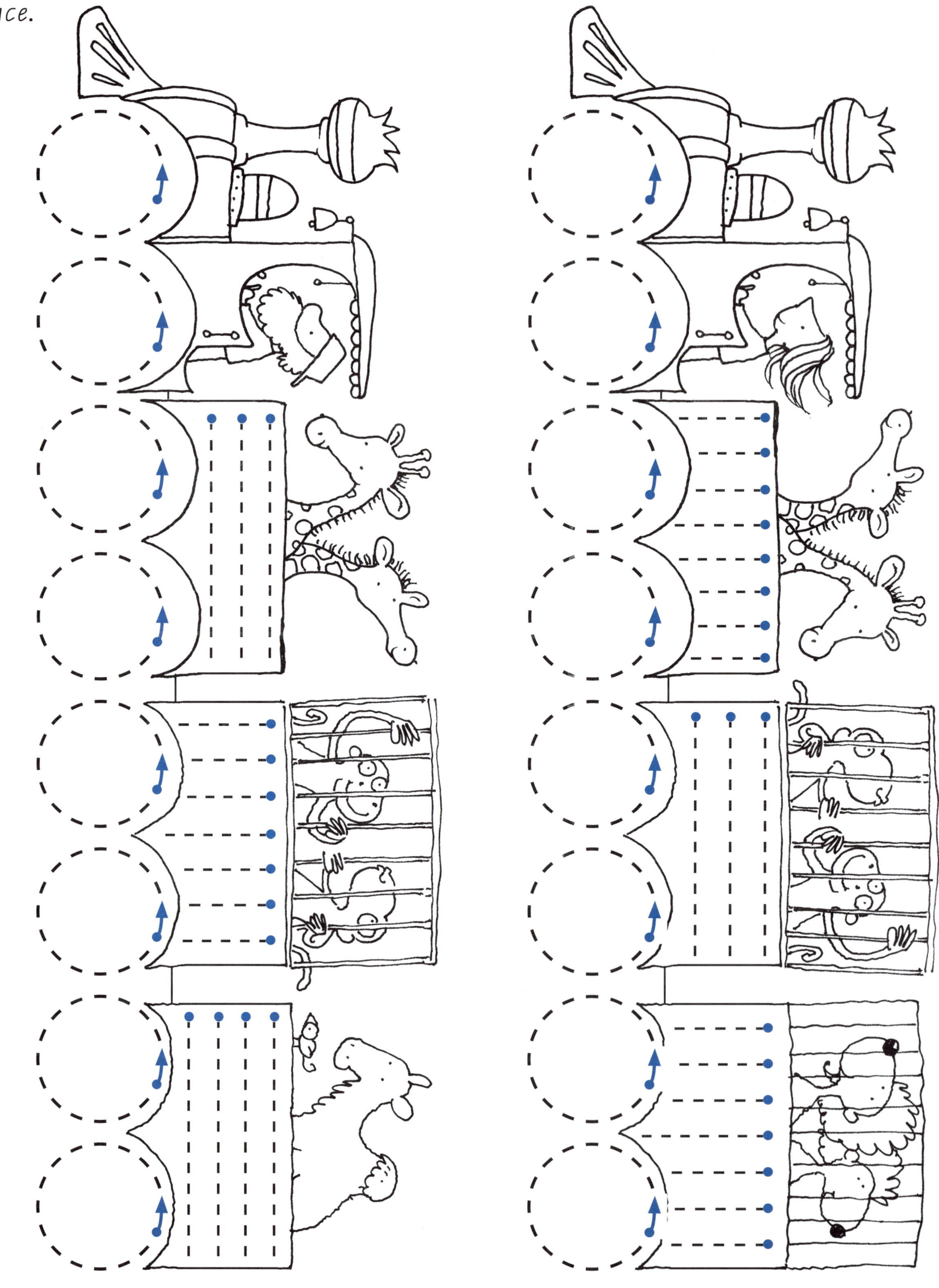

Handwriting: Patterning; downstroke and anticlockwise movements; left to right direction; forming parallel lines; fine motor control.

Trace.

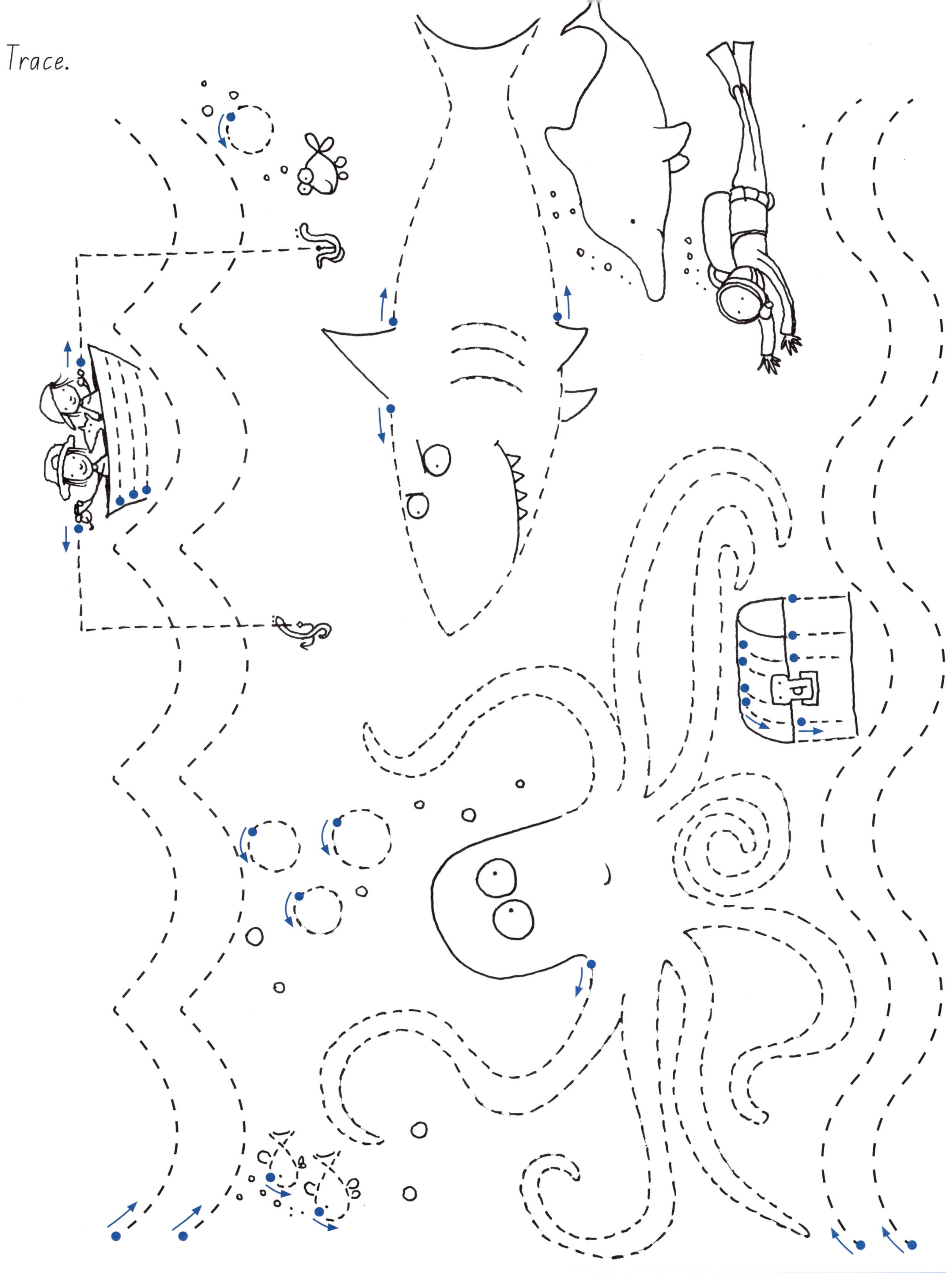

Handwriting: Patterning; downstroke, anticlockwise and clockwise movements; fine motor control.

Chant:

messy monkey

m m m

Trace the pattern.

Trace the pattern. Keep your pencil on the page.

m

Trace the pattern. Turn each pattern into a picture.

Track.

Handwriting: clockwise letter; body letter (m).
Vocabulary on page: messy, monkey.
Extra vocabulary: mat, mop, man, am, mum, men, him, many, munch.

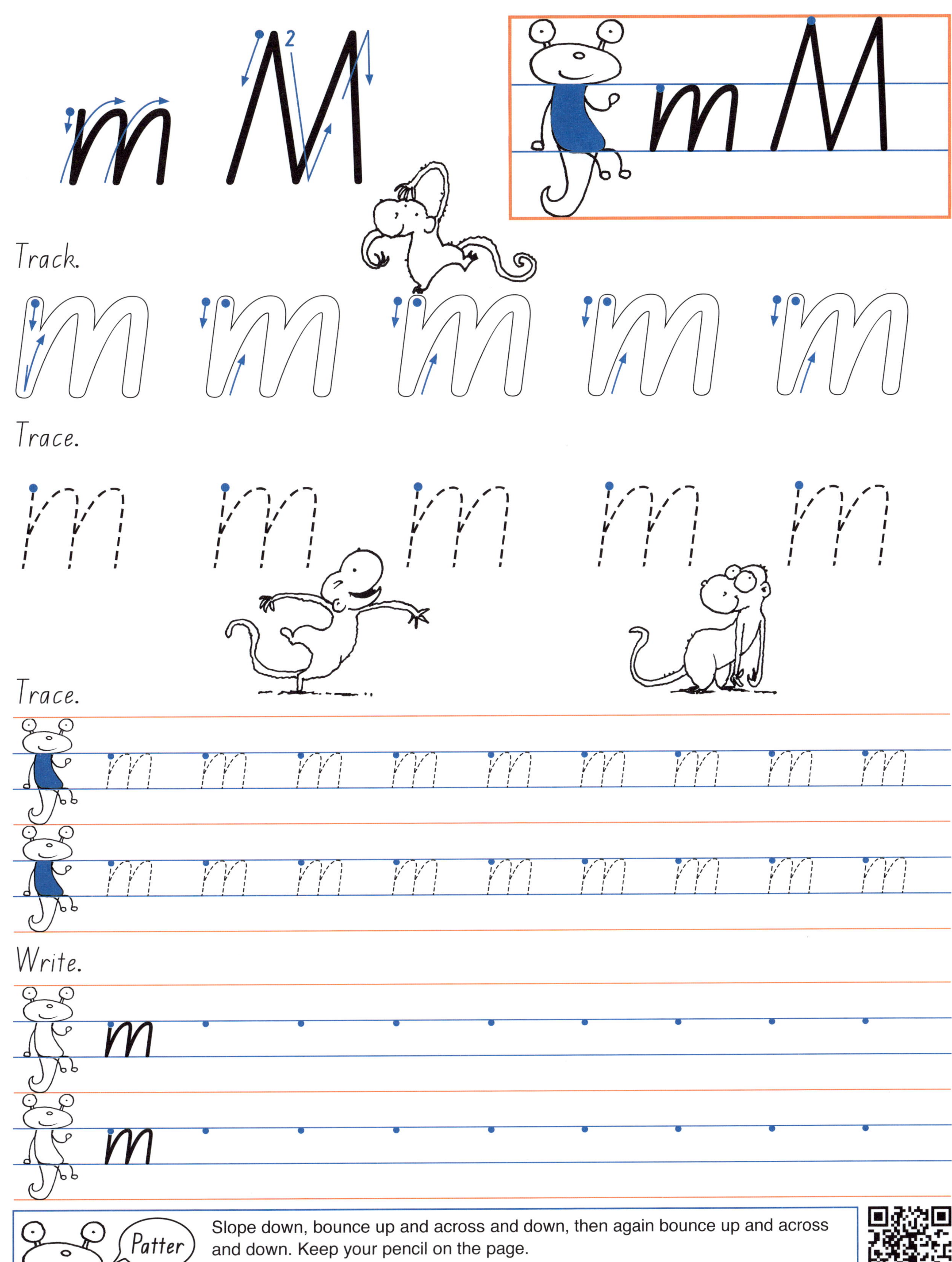

Patter

Slope down, bounce up and across and down, then again bounce up and across and down. Keep your pencil on the page.

Chant:

noisy numbat

n n n

Track the pattern.

Trace the pattern. Keep your pencil on the page.

Copy the pattern. Turn each pattern into a picture.

Track.

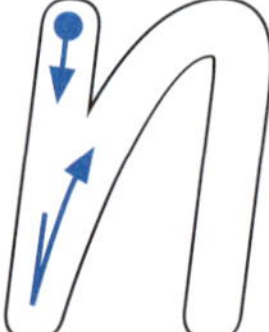

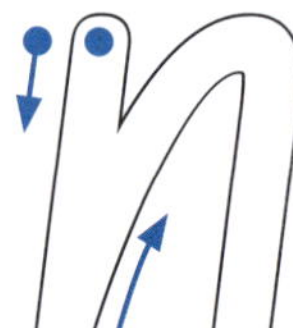

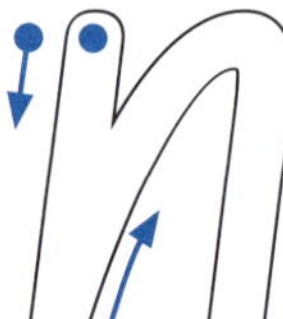

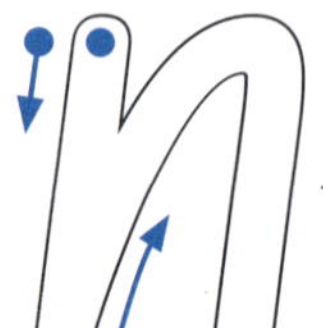

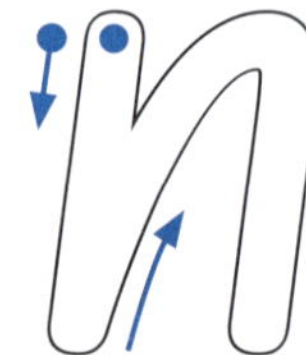

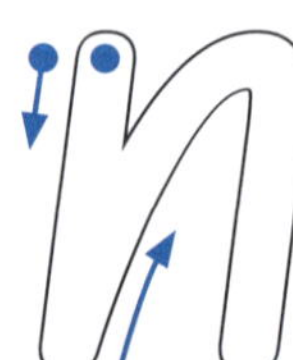

Handwriting: clockwise letter; body letter (n).
Vocabulary on page: noisy, numbat.
Extra vocabulary: no, not, nap, nip, nod, can, sun, run.

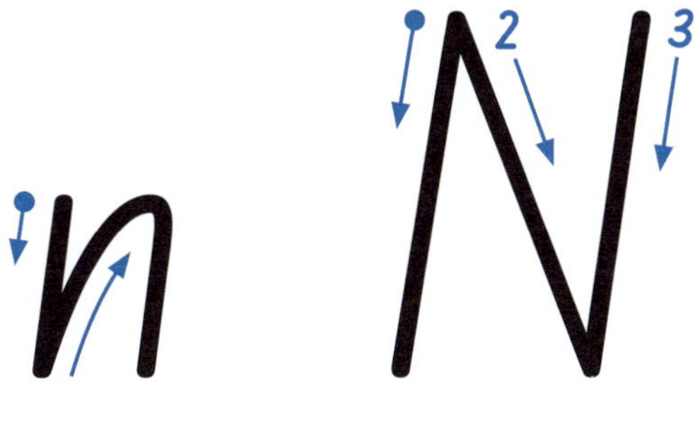

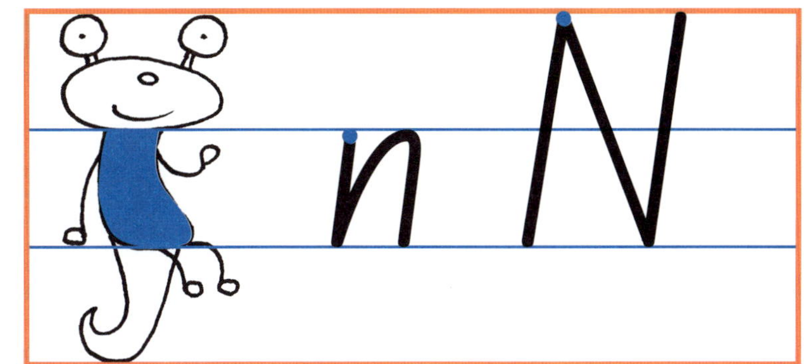

Track.

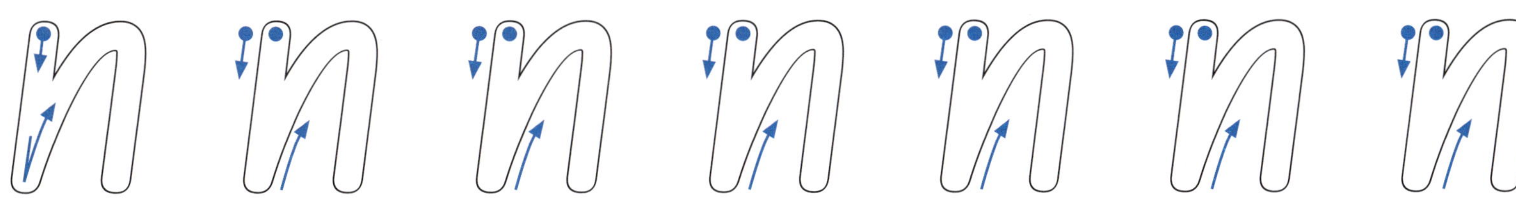

Trace.

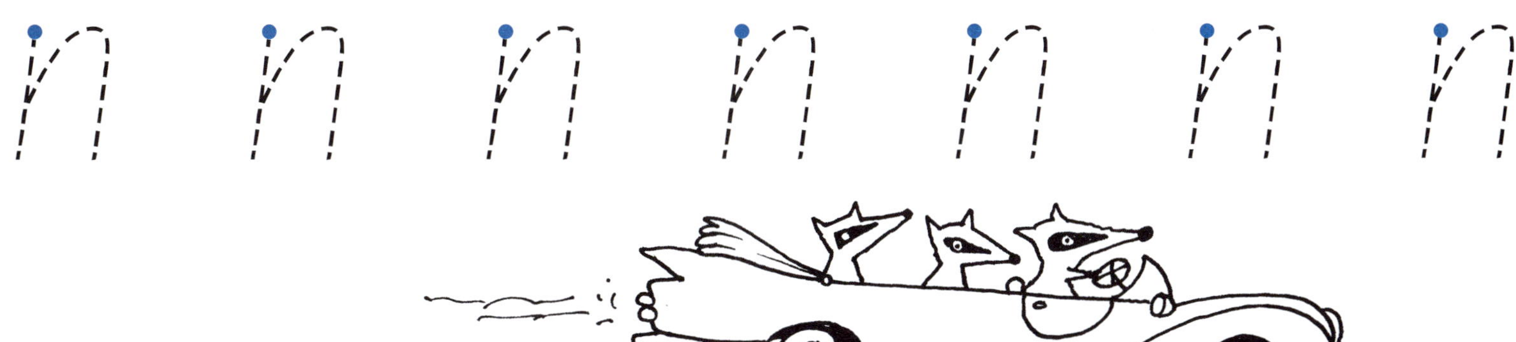

Trace.

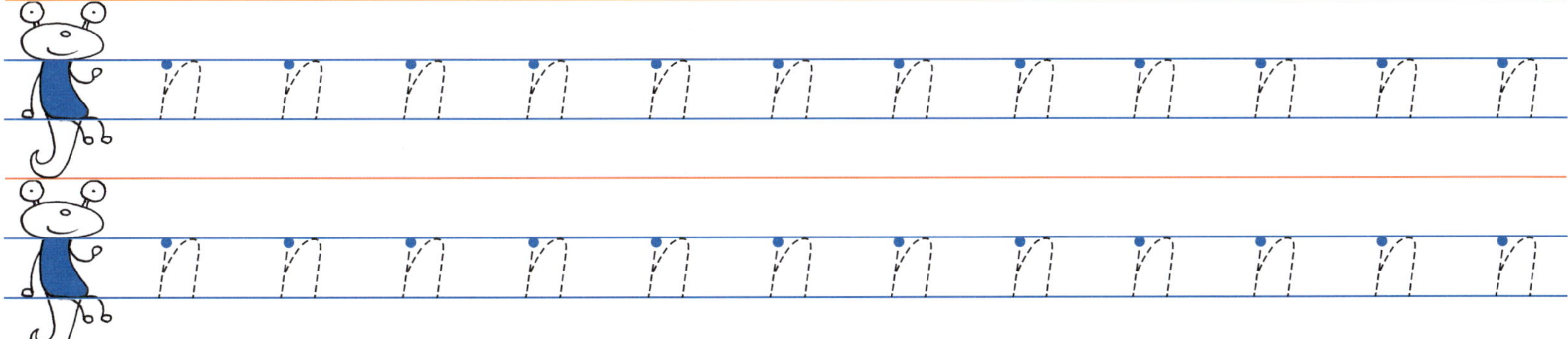

Write.

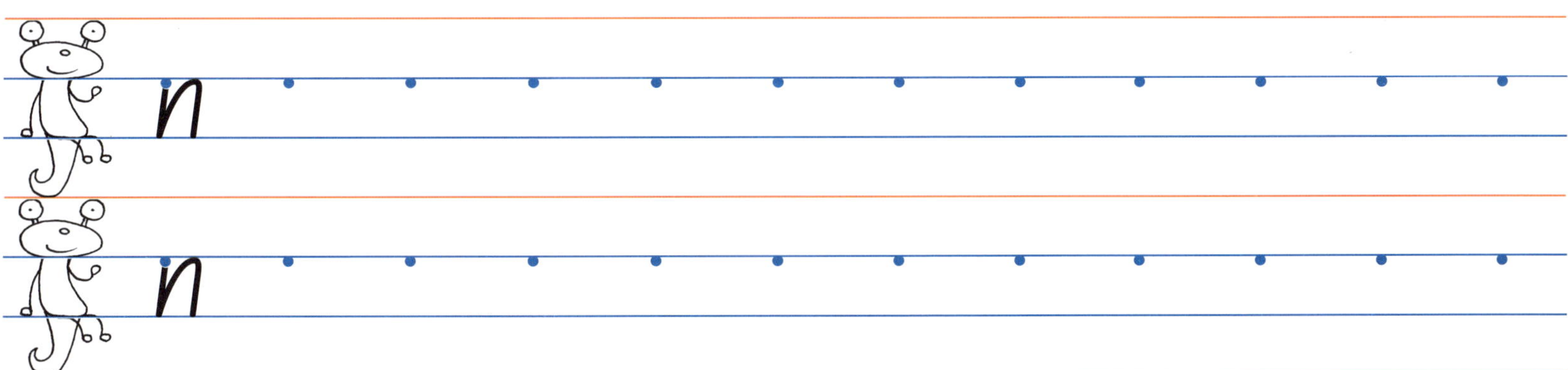

Slope down, then go up and across the top and down again. Keep your pencil on the page.

Chant:

hairy hen

h h h

Trace the pattern.

Trace the pattern. Keep your pencil on the page.

Trace then copy the pattern.

Track.

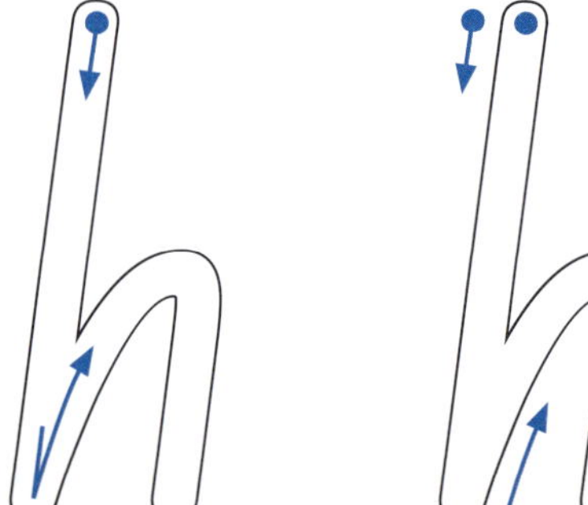

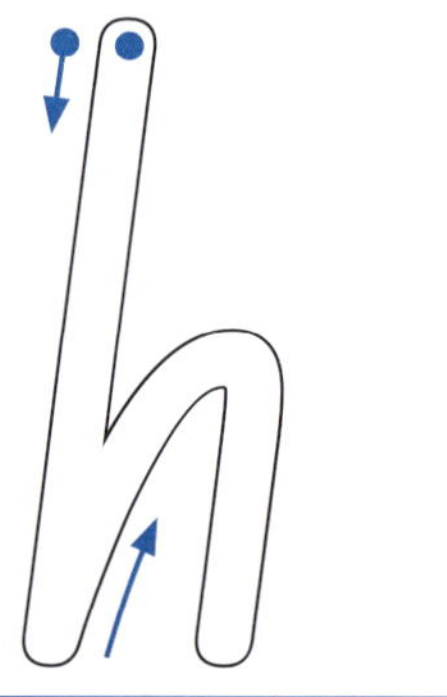
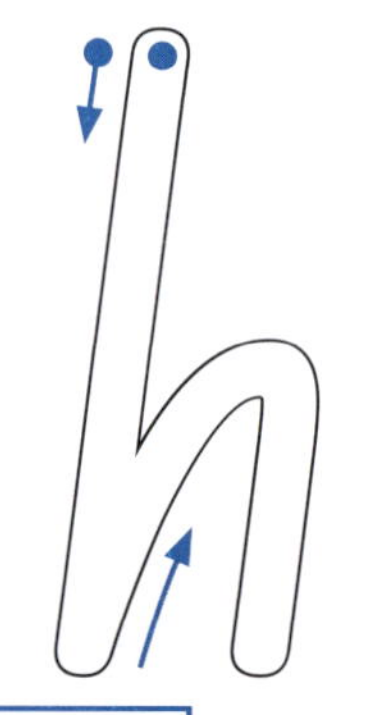

Handwriting: clockwise letter; head and body letter (ascender) (h).
Vocabulary on page: hen, hairy, hay.
Extra vocabulary: hop, help, has, hat, hot, he, she, him, have.

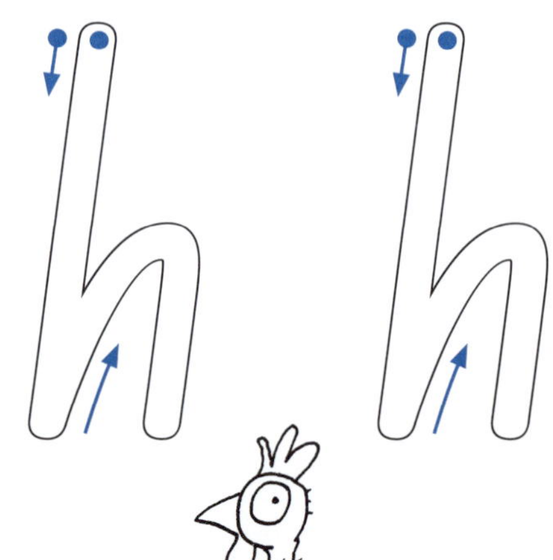

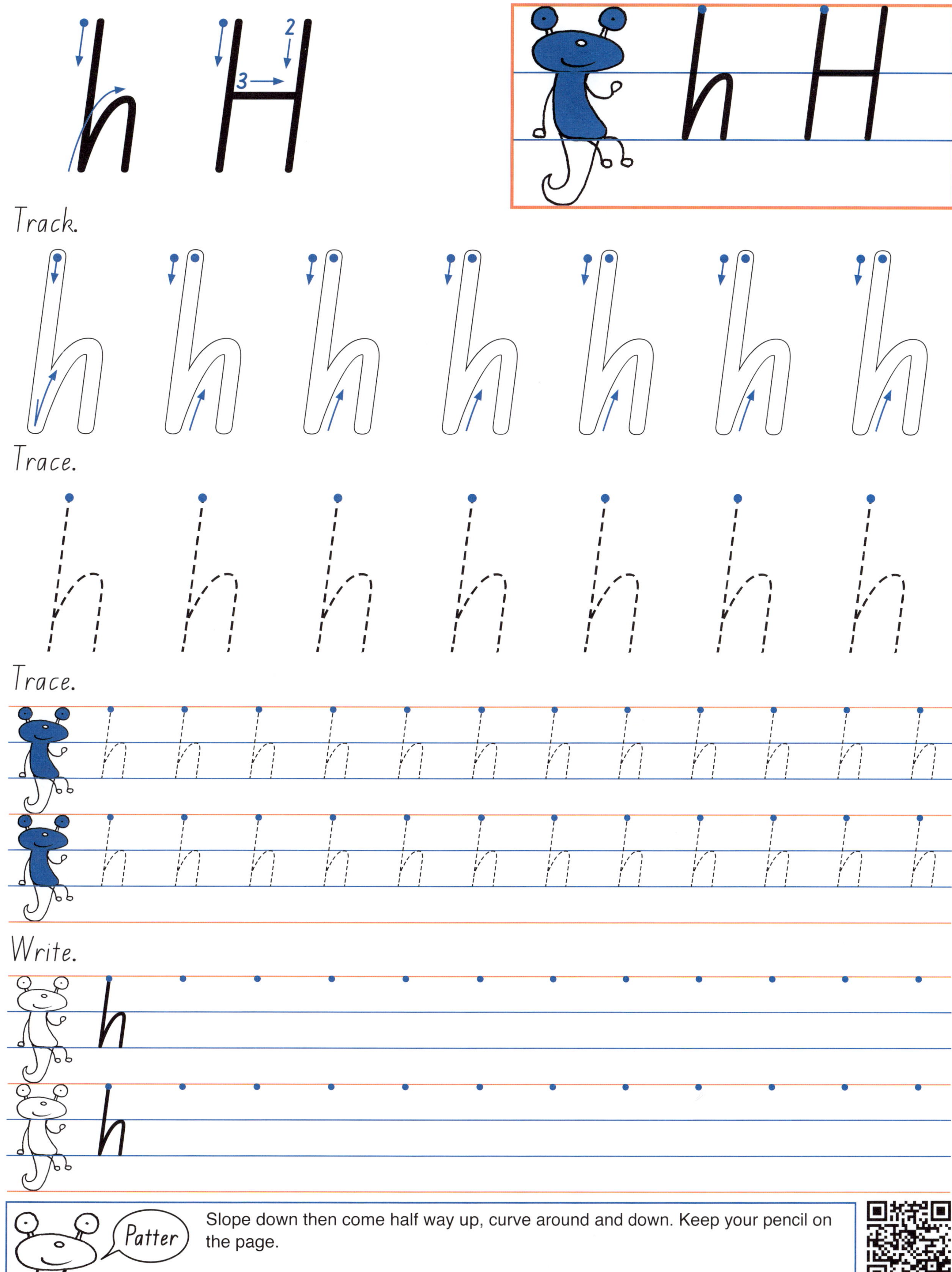
Track.
Trace.
Trace.
Write.
Patter
Slope down then come half way up, curve around and down. Keep your pencil on the page.

Chant:

kind koala
k k k

Trace the pattern. Finish the kites.

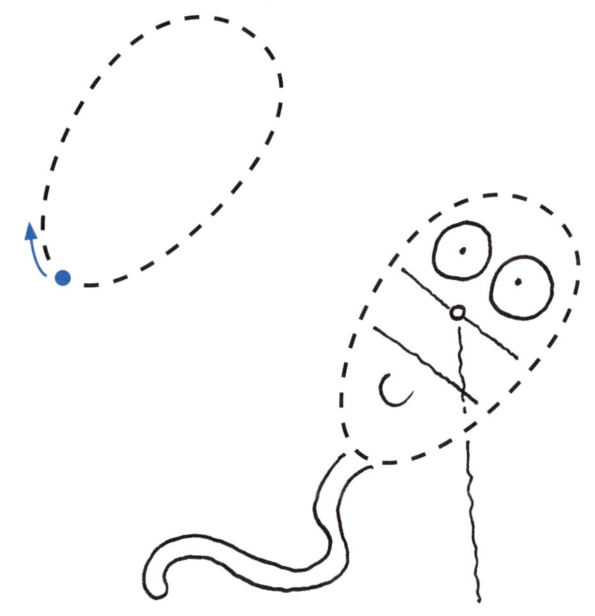

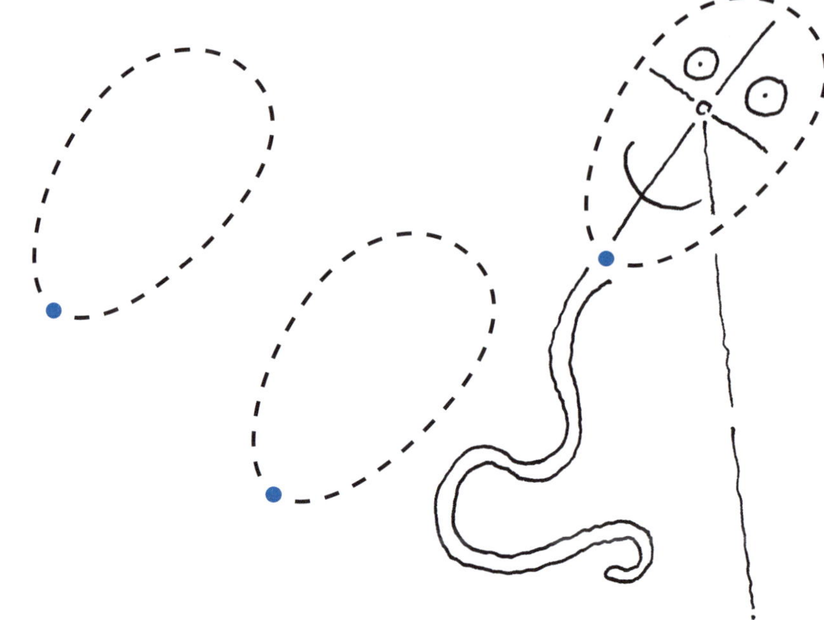

Trace the pattern.

Track.

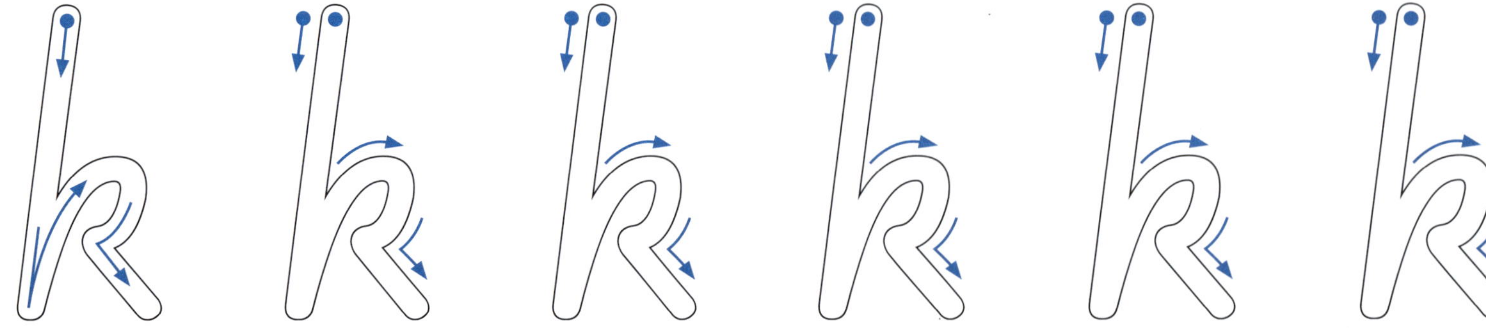

Handwriting: clockwise letter; head and body letter (ascender) (k).
Vocabulary on page: kind, koala, kite.
Extra vocabulary: kit, kitten, king, kangaroo, key.

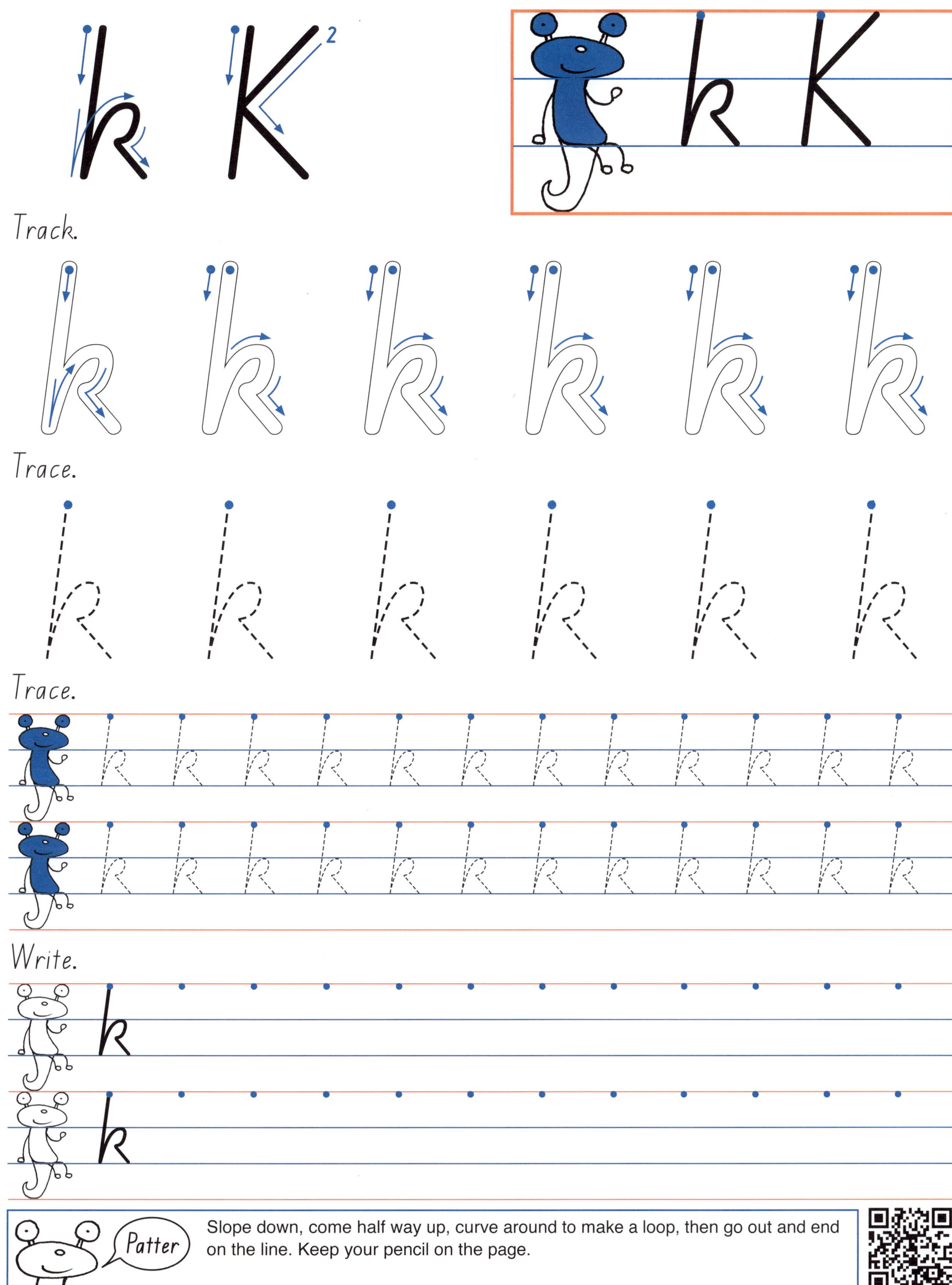

Slope down, come half way up, curve around to make a loop, then go out and end on the line. Keep your pencil on the page.

Chant:

pretty pig
p p p

Trace the pattern. Keep your pencil on the page.

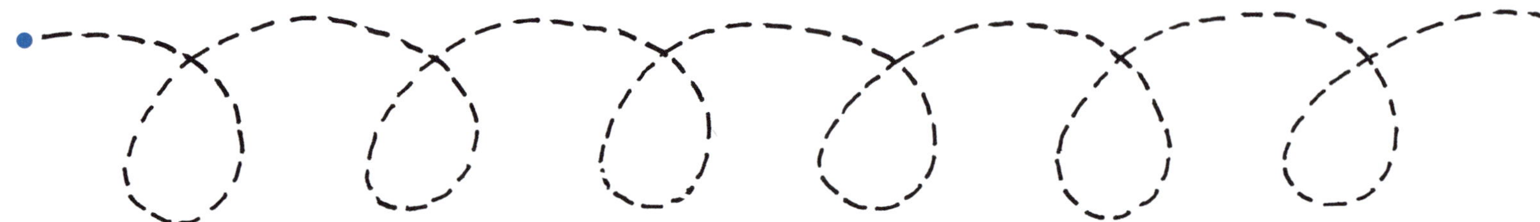

Trace the patterns.

Copy the pattern.

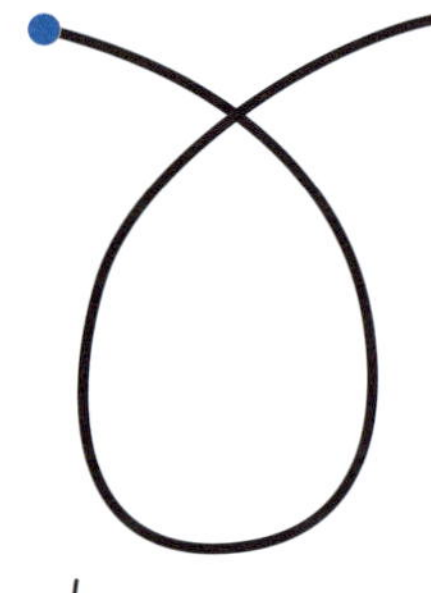

Track.

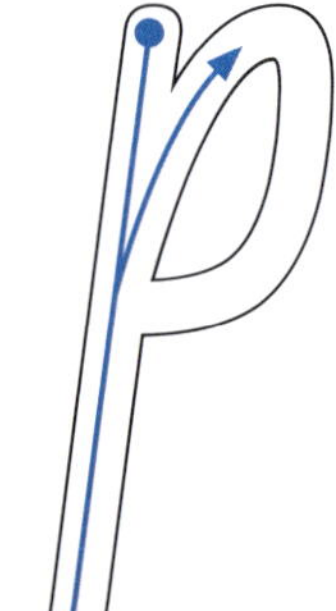
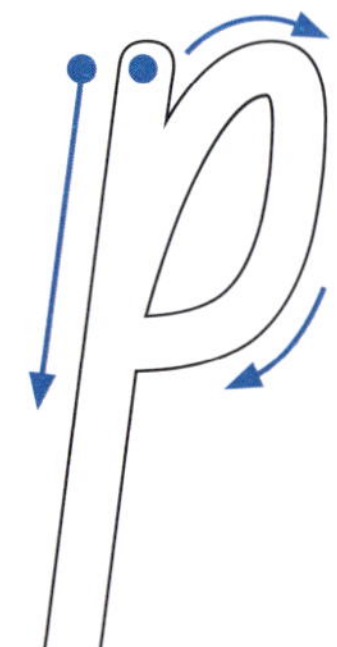
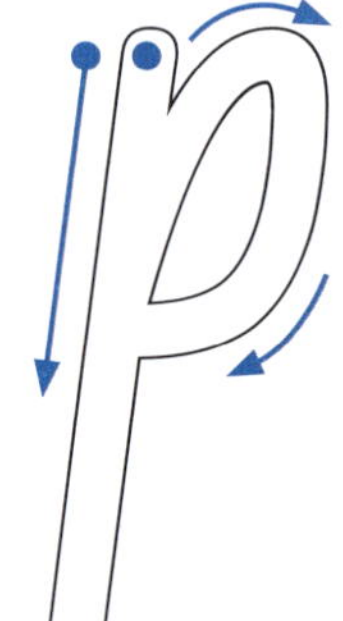
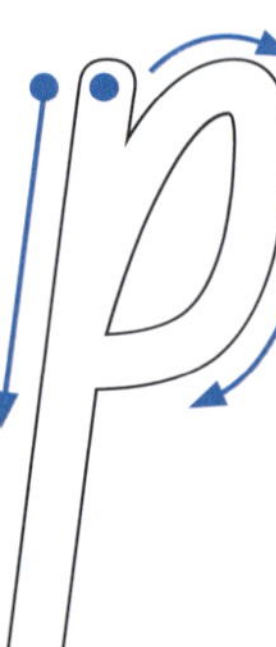
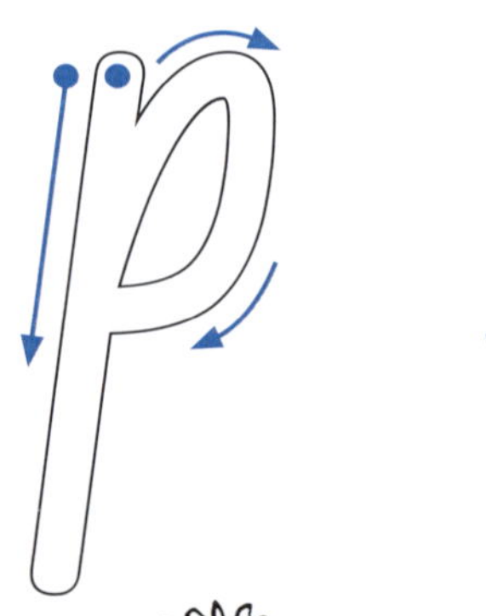
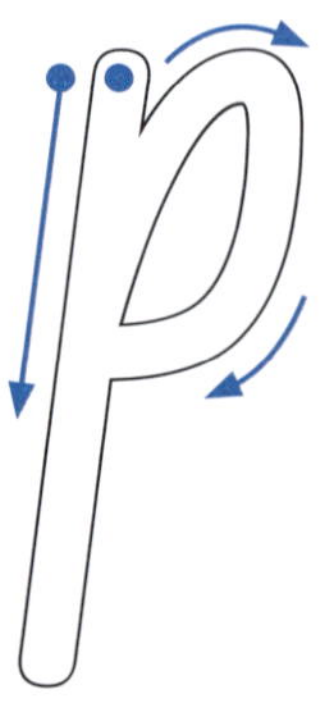

Handwriting: clockwise letter; body and tail letter (descender) (p).
Vocabulary on page: pig, pretty.
Extra vocabulary: pat, pot, put, pan, pop, map, nip, top, pink.

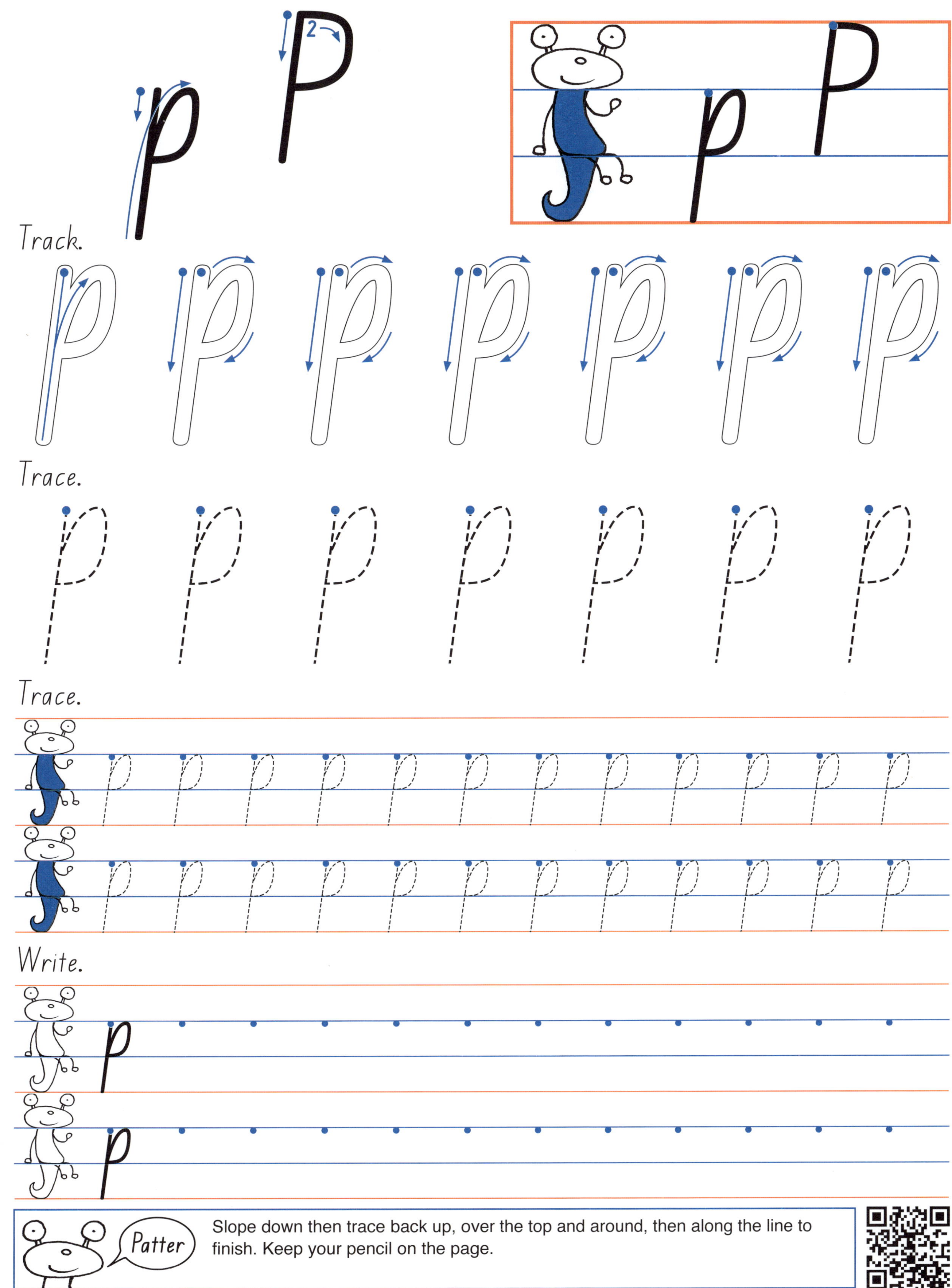
Track.
Trace.
Trace.
Write.
Patter
Slope down then trace back up, over the top and around, then along the line to finish. Keep your pencil on the page.

Chant:

bouncy bear
b b b

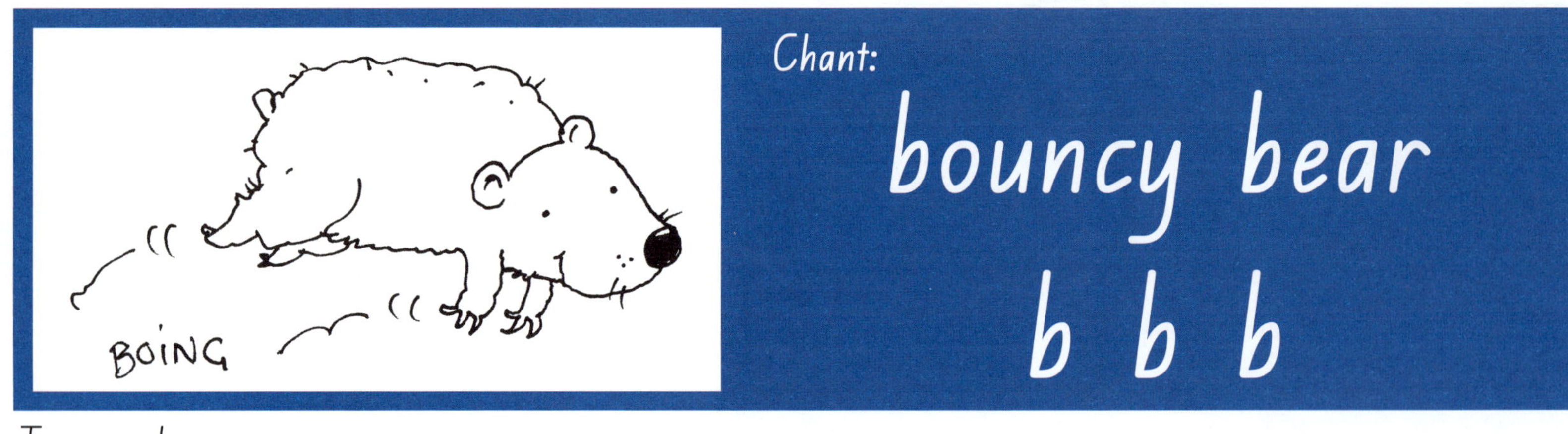

Trace the pattern.

Trace the pattern.

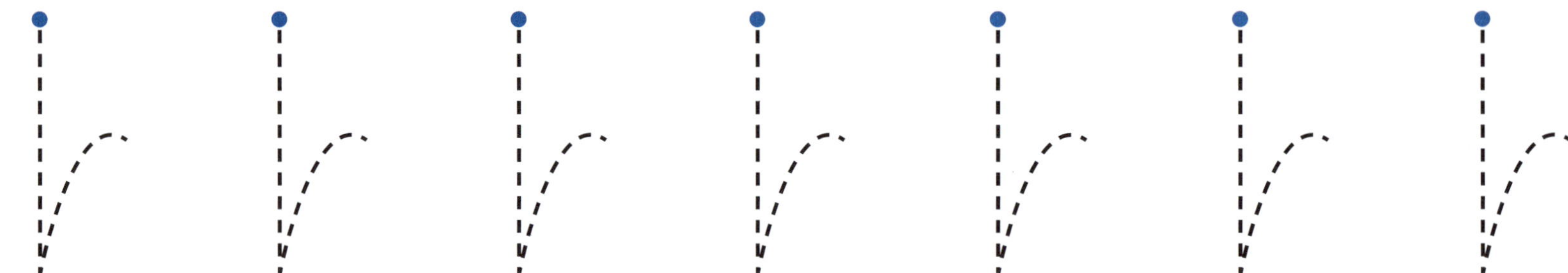

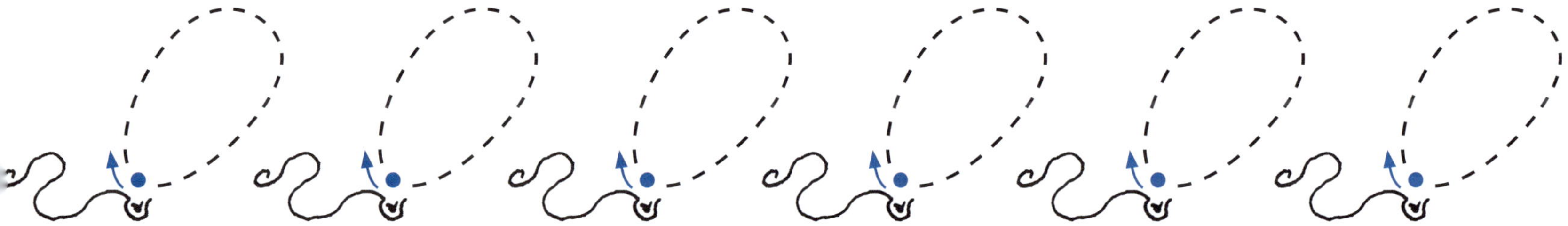

Find b.

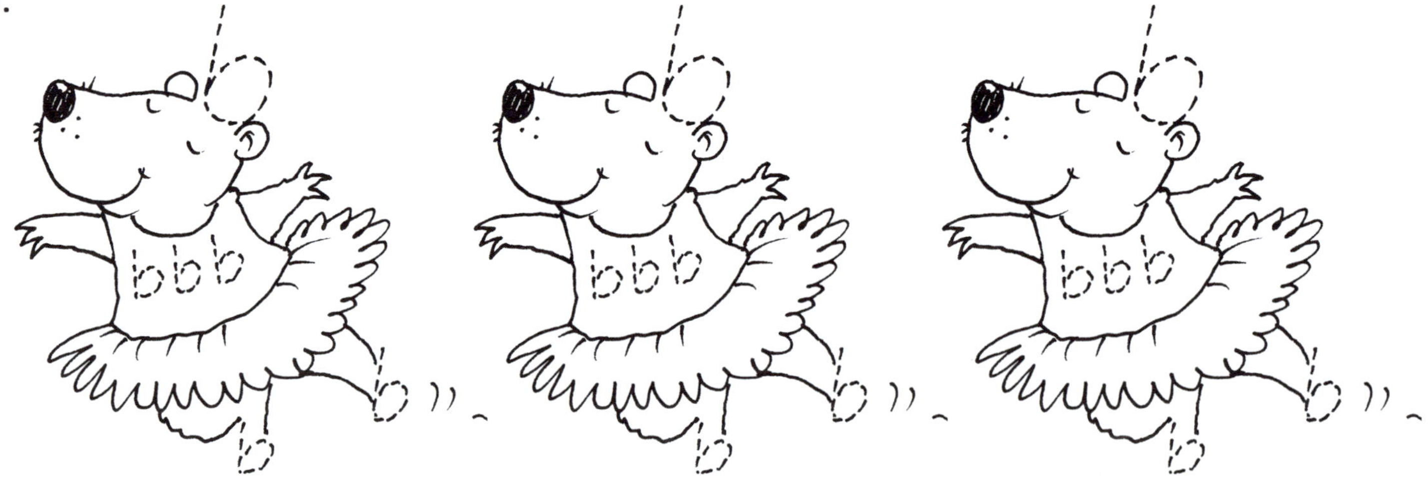

Track.

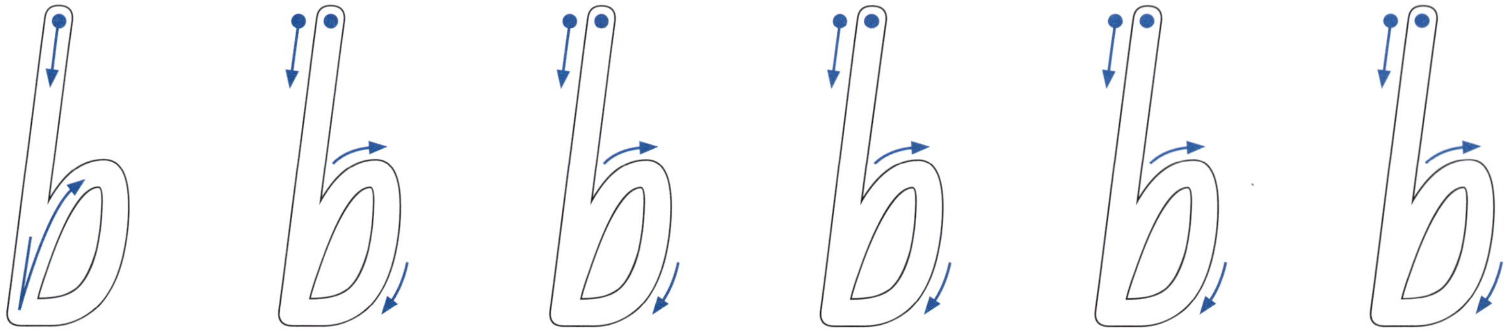

Handwriting: clockwise letter; head and body letter (ascender) (b).
Vocabulary on page: bear, balloon, ballet, bouncy.
Extra vocabulary: be, bee, by, bat, big, bed, but, bug.

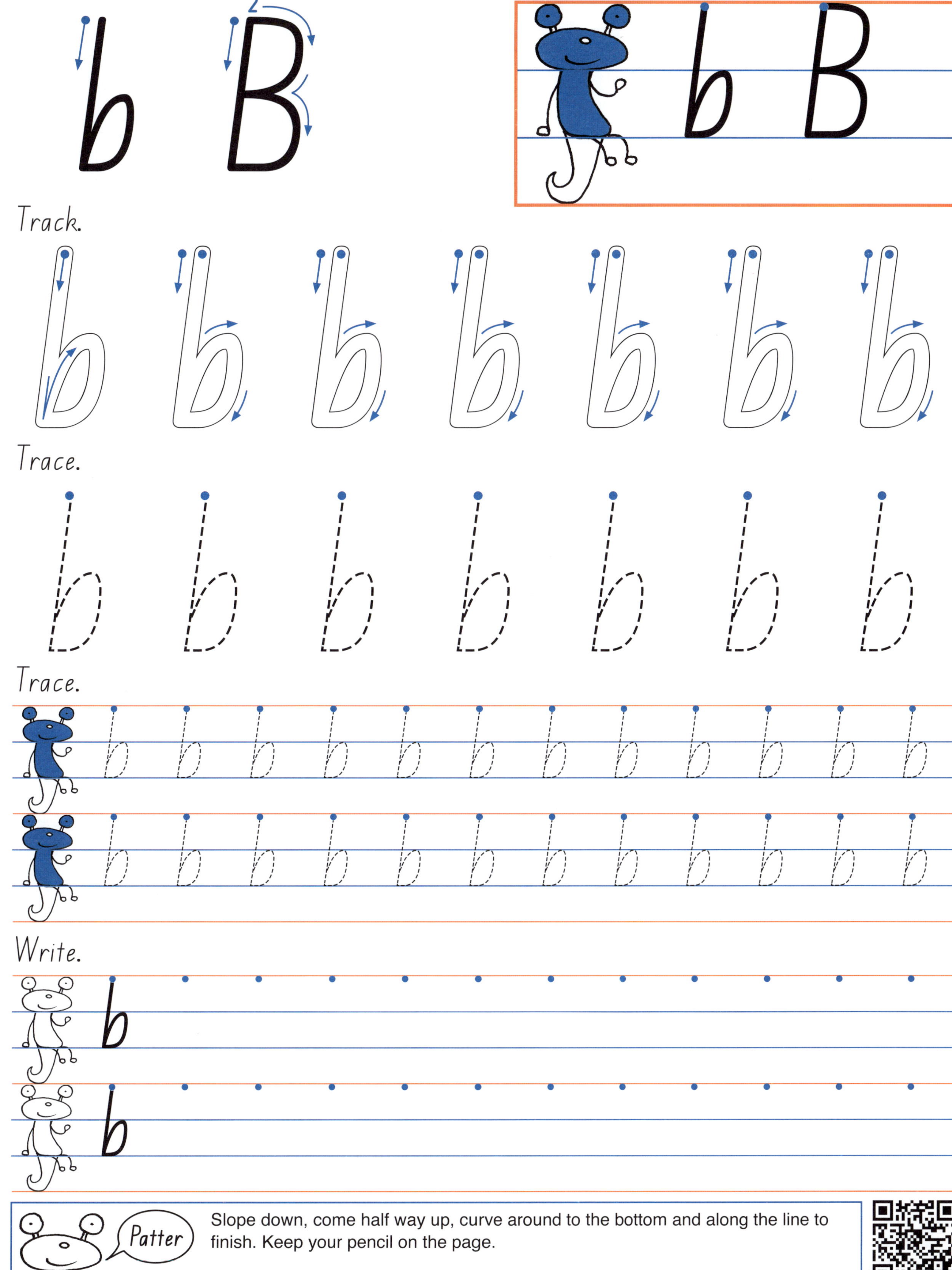

Slope down, come half way up, curve around to the bottom and along the line to finish. Keep your pencil on the page.

Chant:

rapid rat

r r r

Trace the pattern.

Find r.

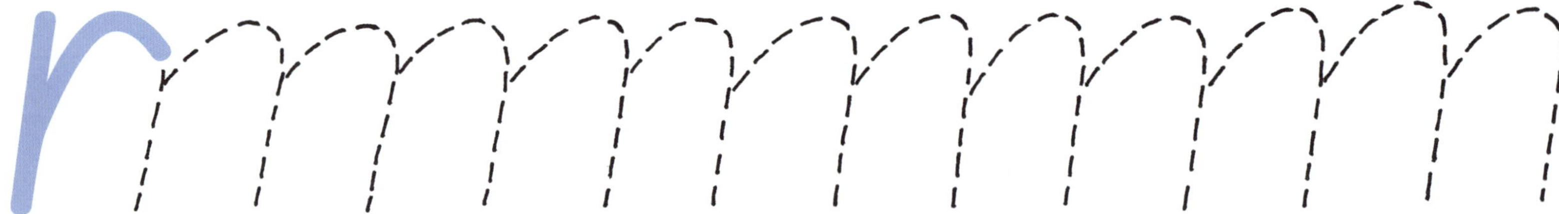

Track.

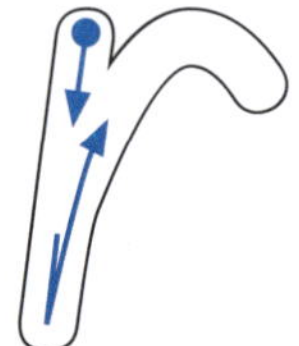 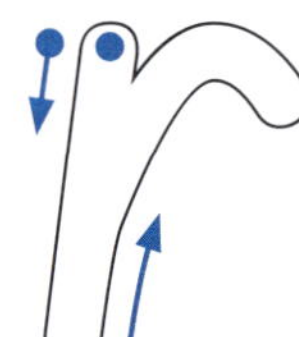 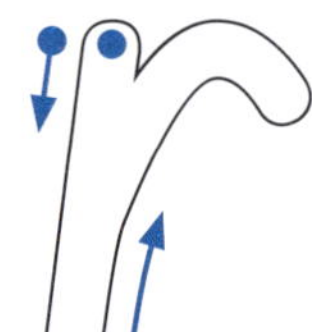 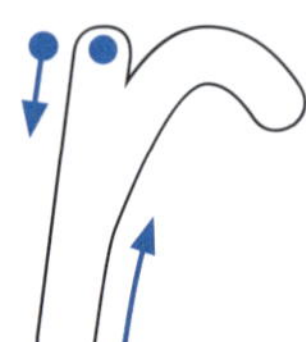 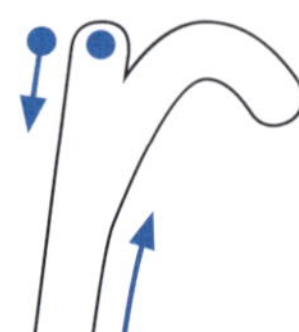 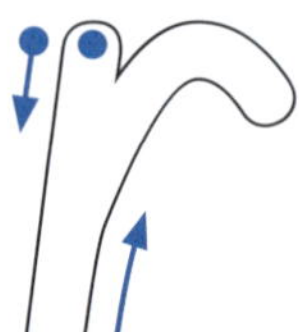

Handwriting: clockwise letter; body letter (r).
Vocabulary on page: rat, race, rapid.
Extra vocabulary: rip, run, ran, raft.

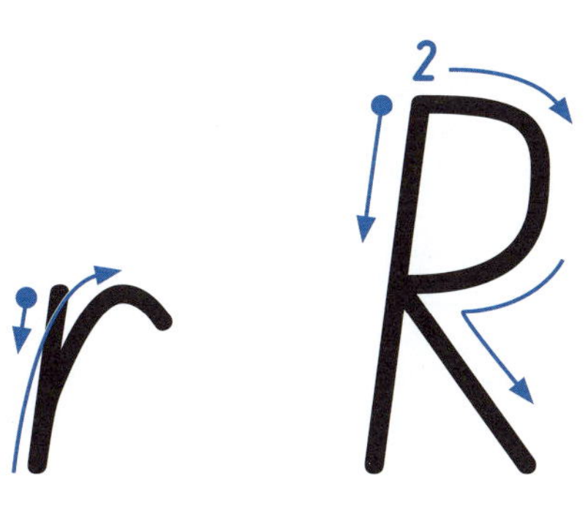

Track.

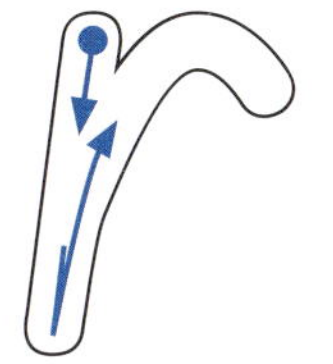 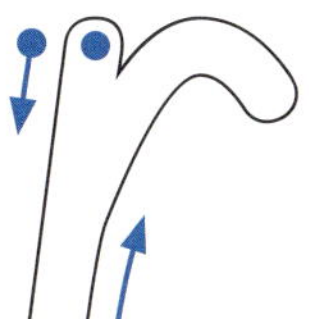 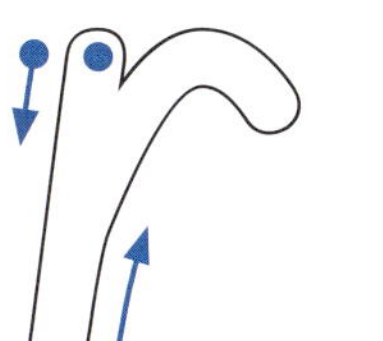 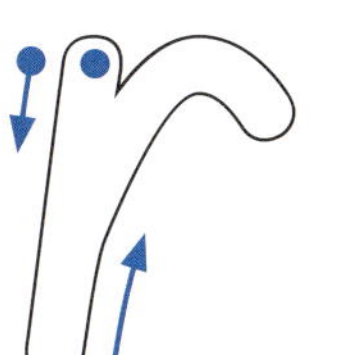 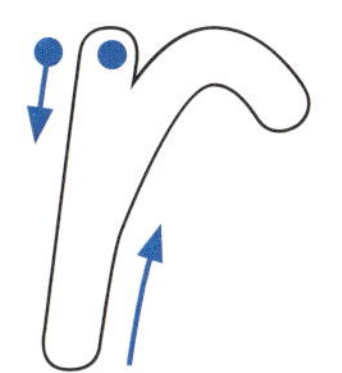 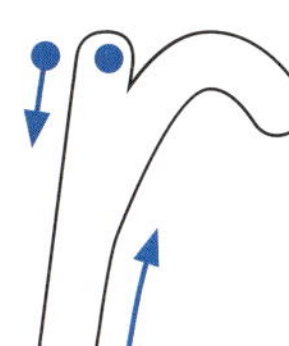 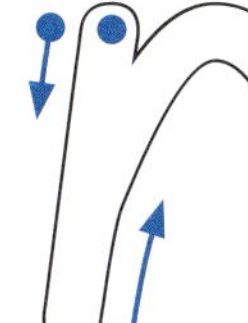

Trace.

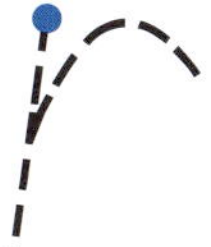 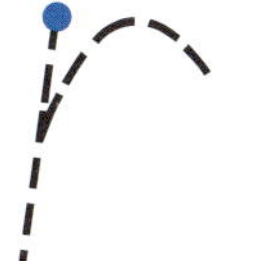 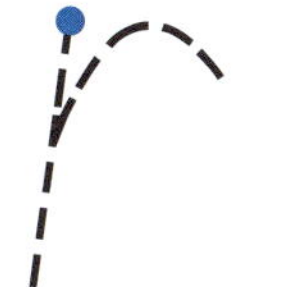 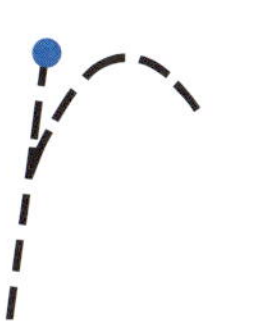 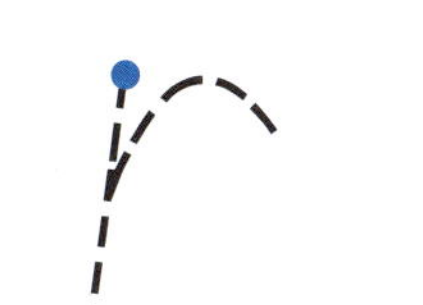  

Trace.

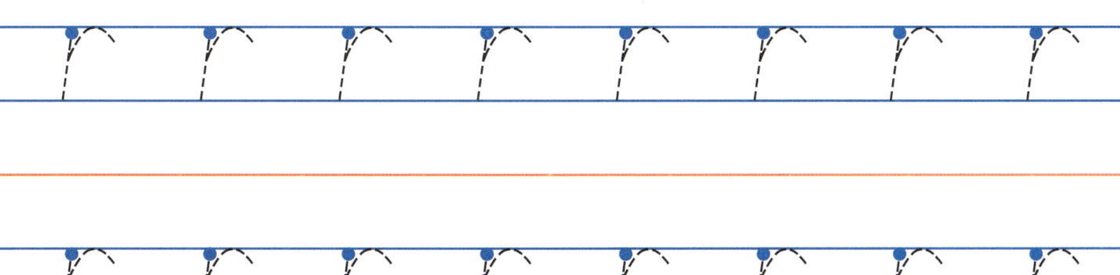

Write.

Slope down then retrace up, over the top and finish with a small downward stroke. Keep your pencil on the page.

Chant:

jiggly jellyfish
j j j

Trace the pattern.

Trace the pattern. Keep your pencil on the page.

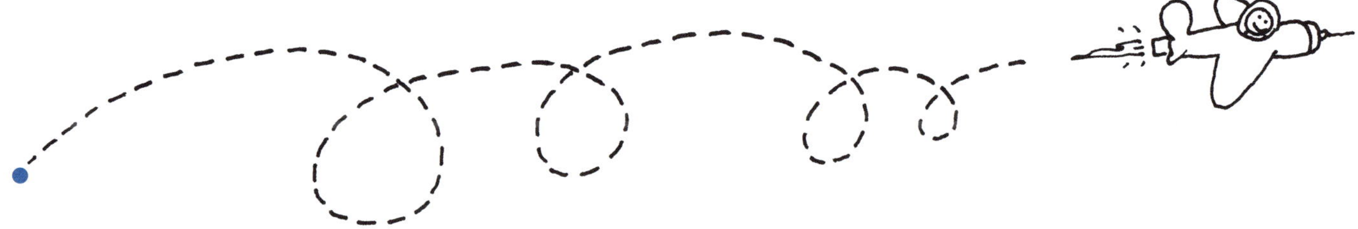

Trace the pattern. Keep your pencil on the page.

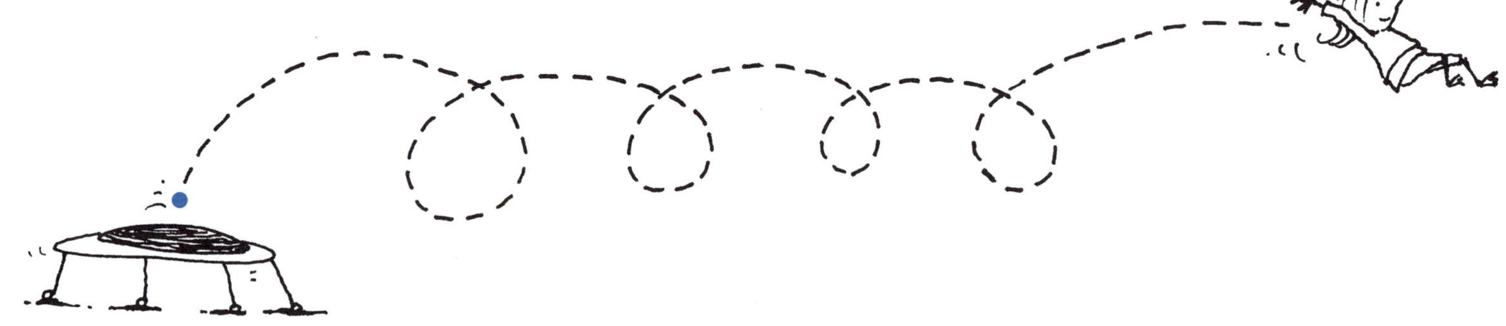

Track.

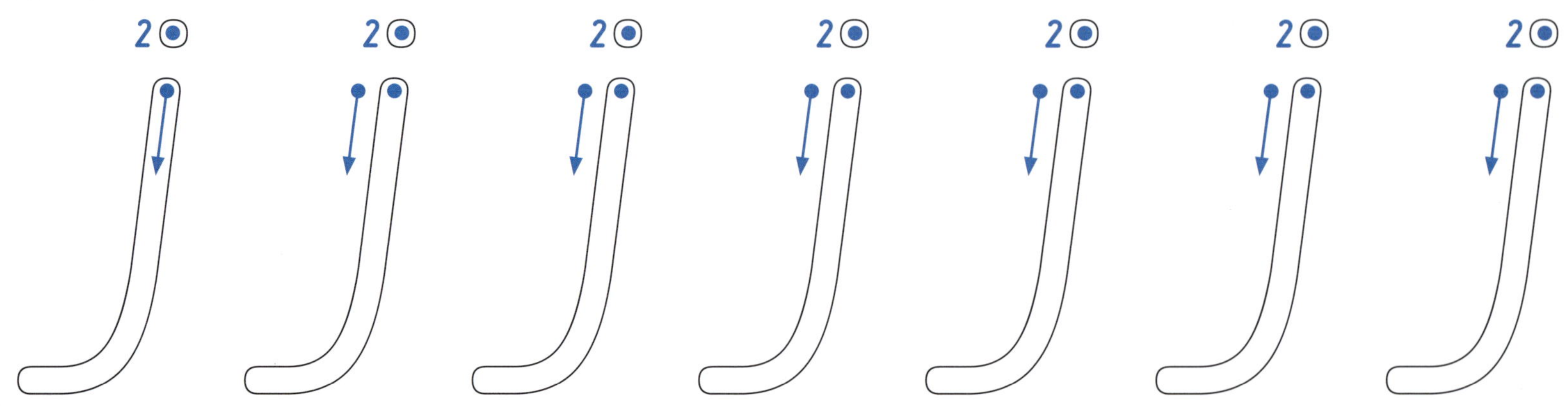

Handwriting: clockwise letter; body and tail letter (descender) (j).
Vocabulary on page: jet, jump, jellyfish, jiggly.
Extra vocabulary: job, just.

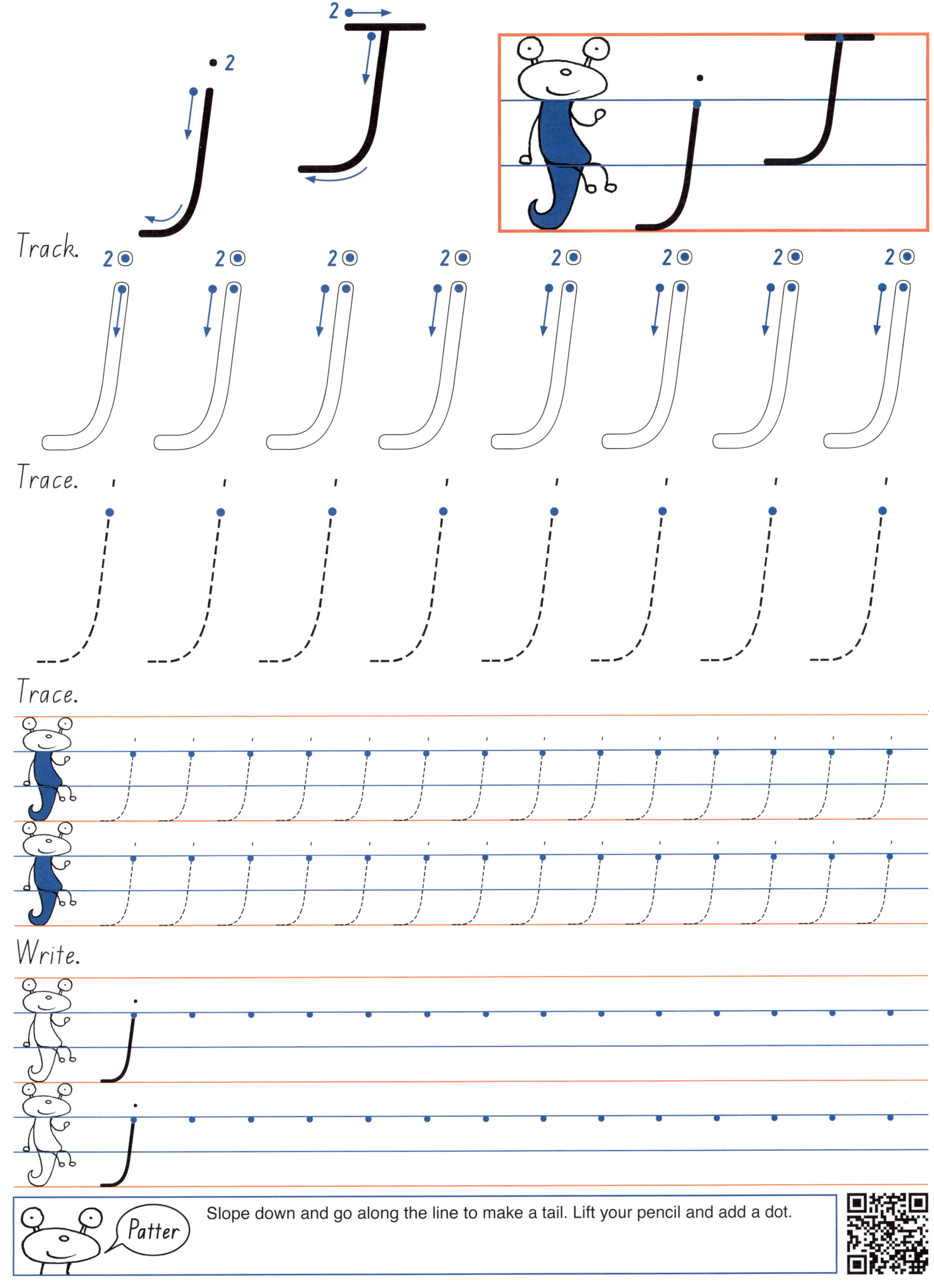

Slope down and go along the line to make a tail. Lift your pencil and add a dot.

Chant:

itchy iguana

i i i

Trace the pattern.

Trace.

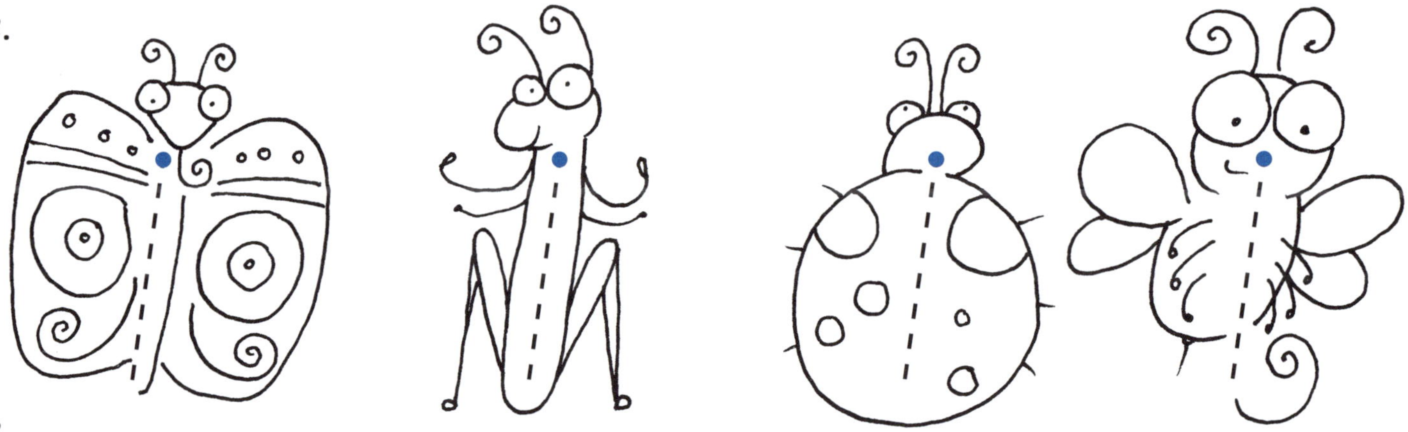

Trace.

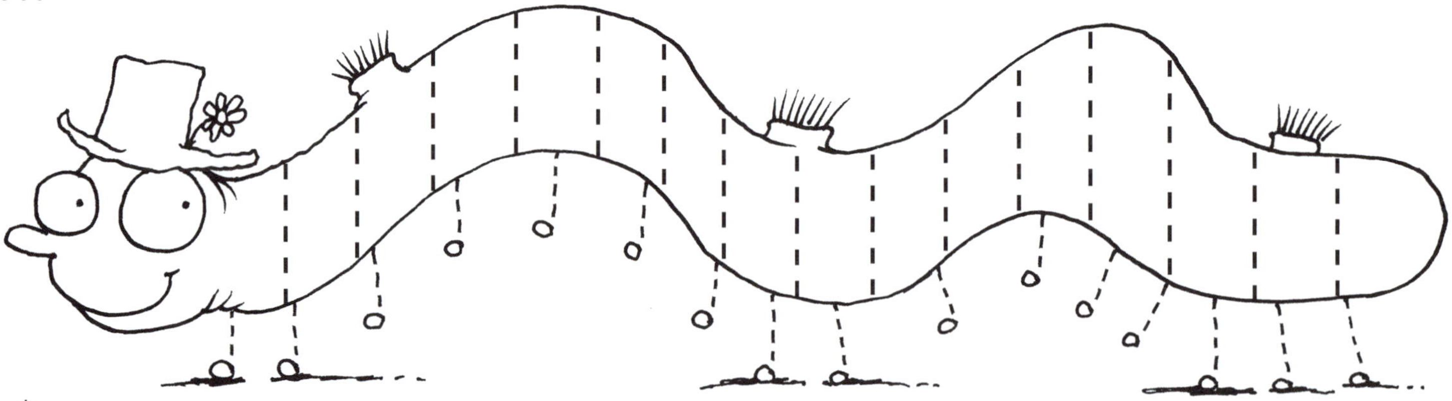

Track.

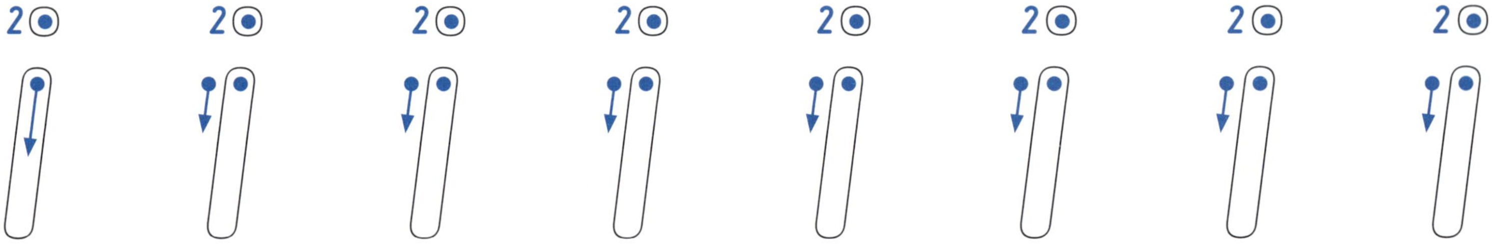

2 2 2 2 2 2 2 2

Handwriting: straight-line letter; body letter (i).
Vocabulary on page: insect, itchy, iguana.
Extra vocabulary: I, is, it, in, if, six, will, sit, lip.

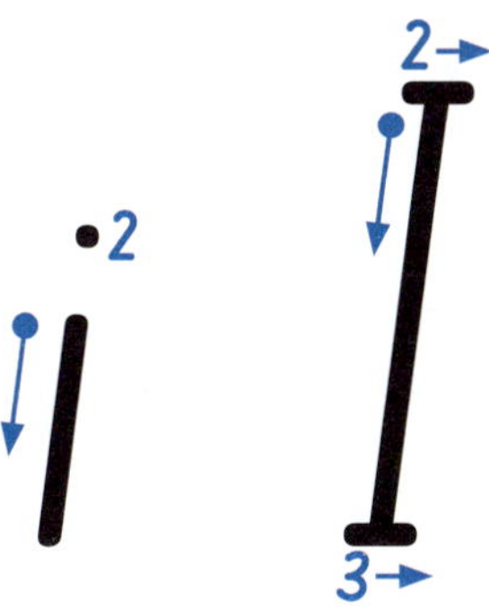

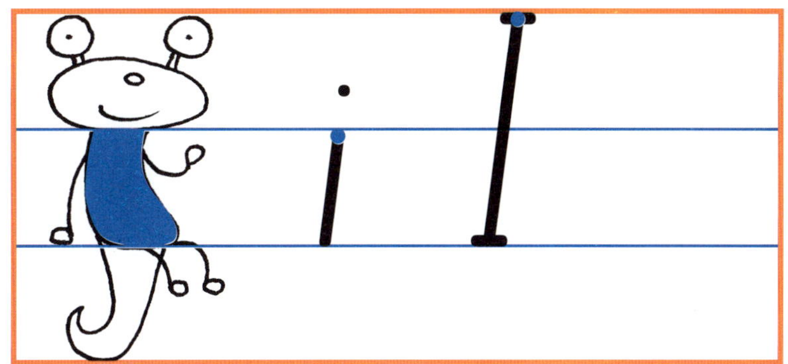

Trace the pattern. Keep your pencil on the page.

Copy the pattern.

illi

Trace.

Write.

i

i

Slope down. Lift your pencil and add a dot.

Chant:

tidy turtle

t t t

Trace the pattern.

Find and write t.

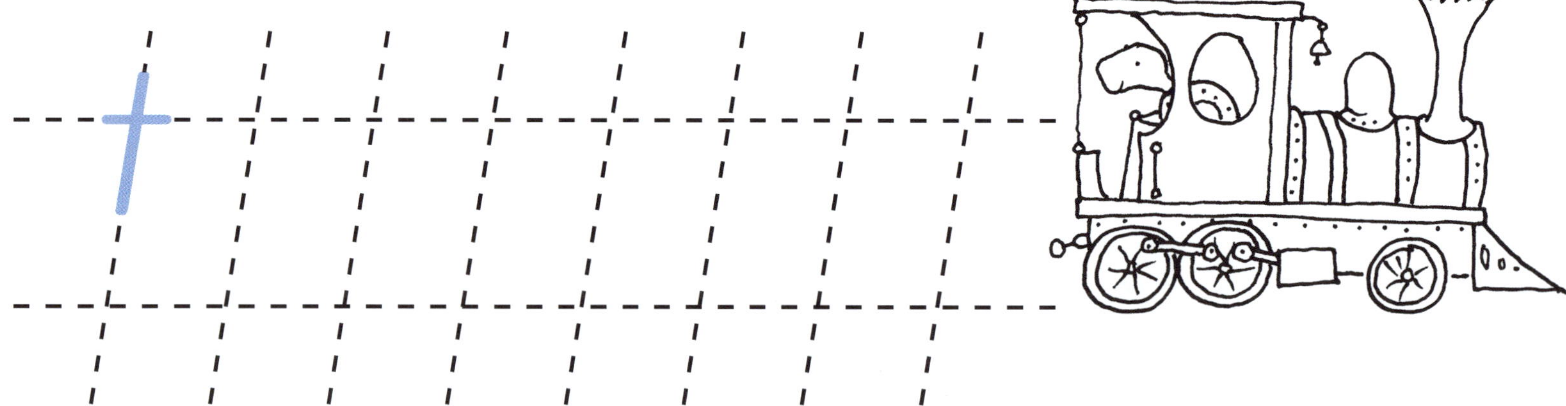

Track.

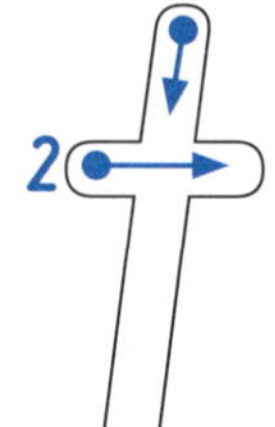

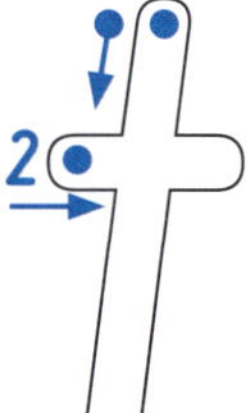

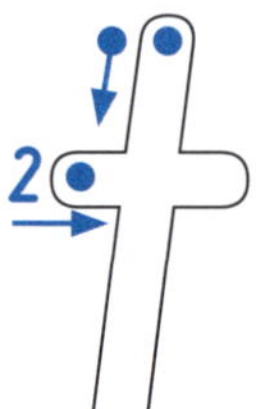

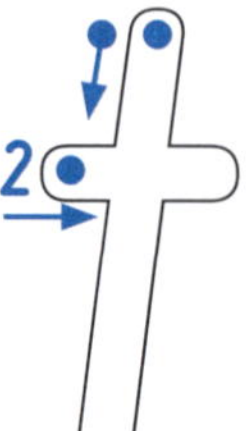

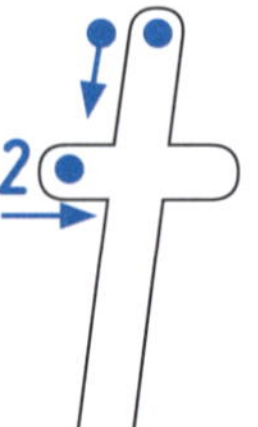

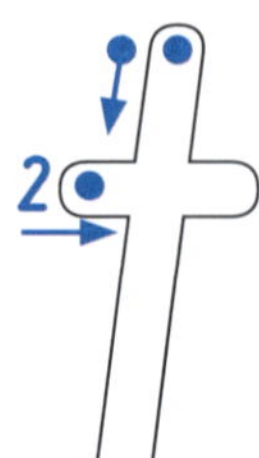

Handwriting: straight-line letter; head and body letter (ascender) (t).
Vocabulary on page: track, train, tree, turtle, tidy, tortoise.
Extra vocabulary: tap, tip, ten, it, at, hot, get, pet, net.

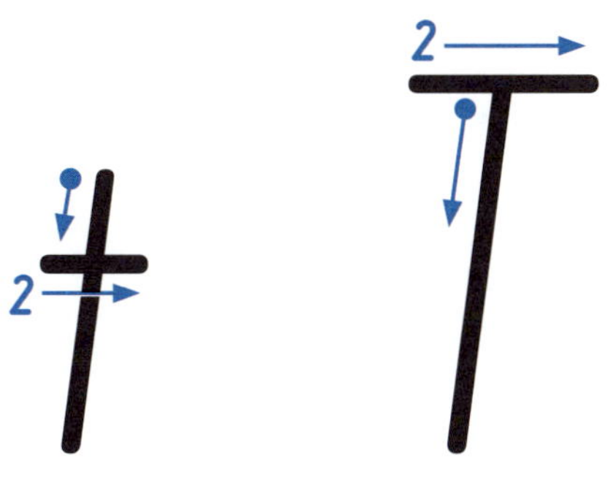

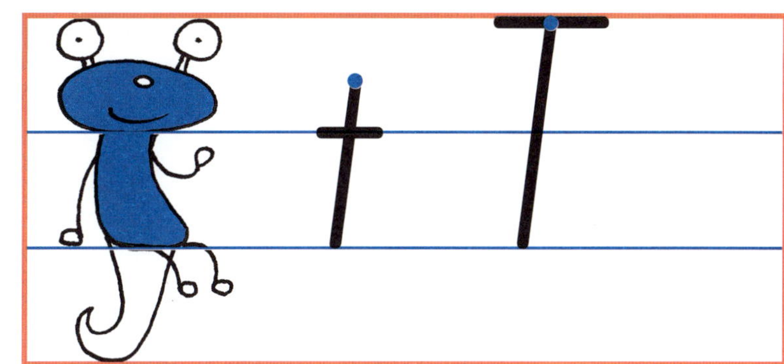

Track.

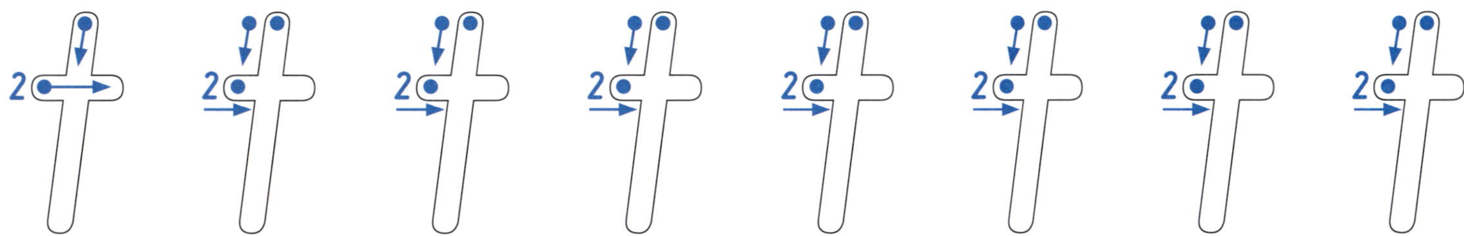

Trace.

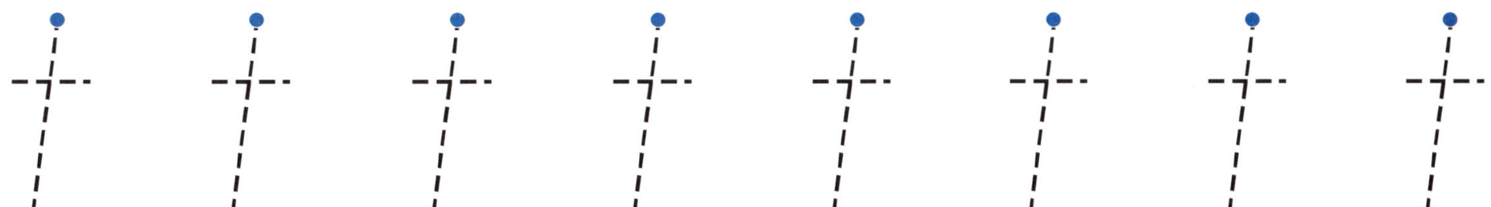

Trace.

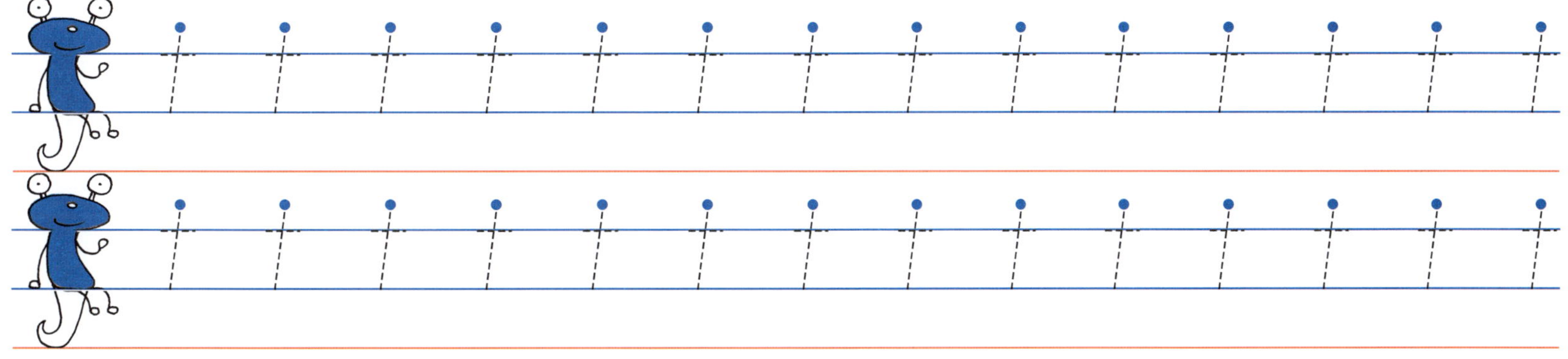

Write.

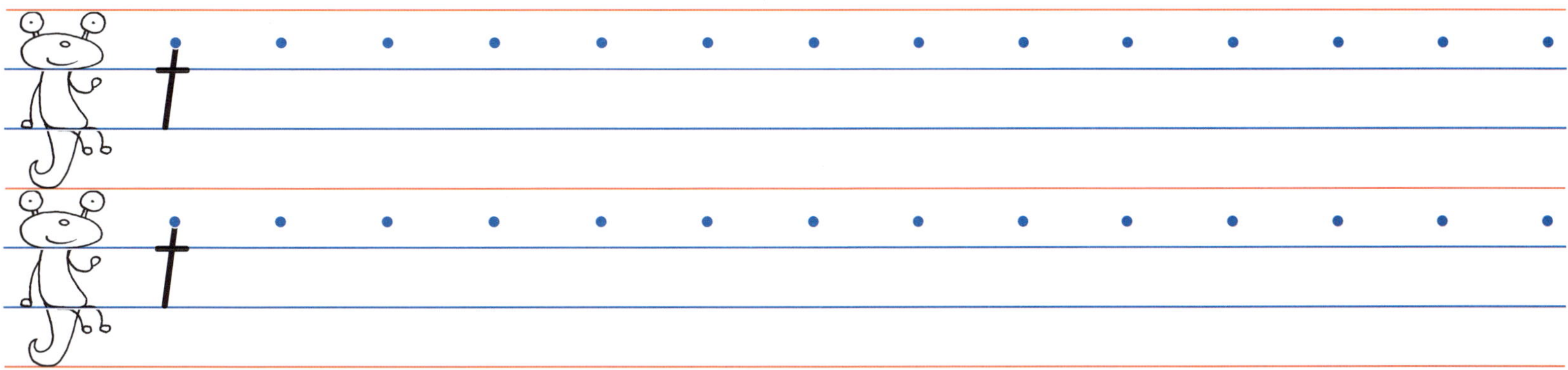

Start half way between the lines. Slope down. Lift your pencil and make a cross.

Chant:

lazy lion

l l l

Trace the pattern.

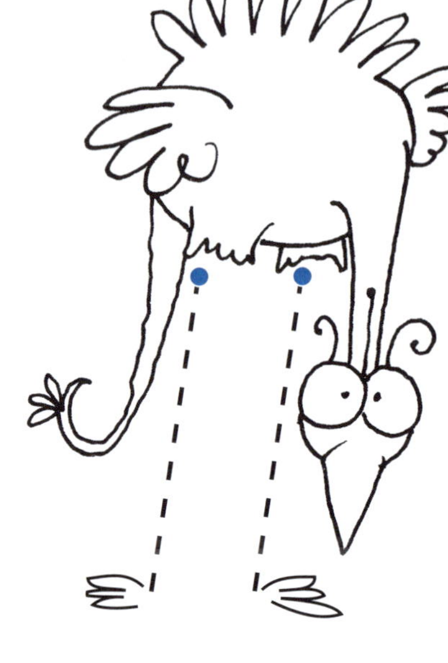

Trace the pattern.

Track.

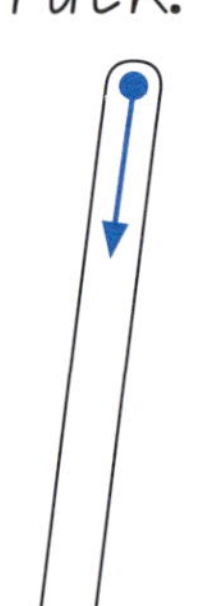

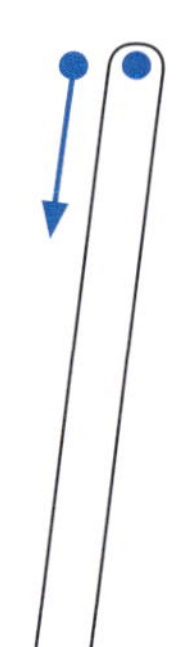
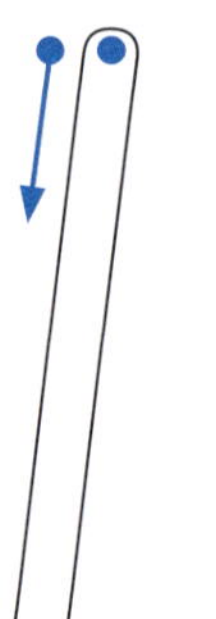
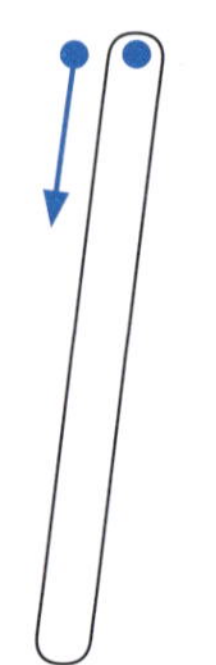
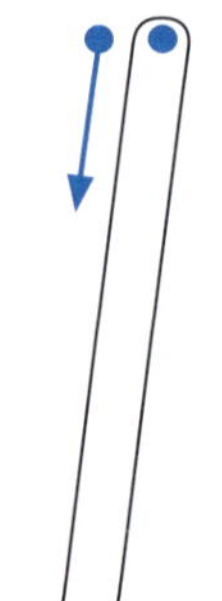
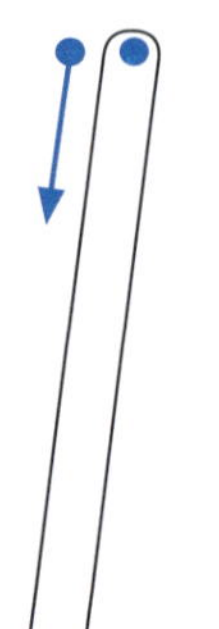
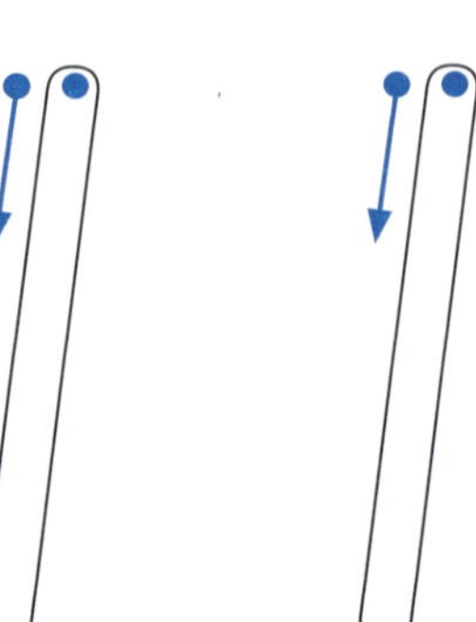

Handwriting: straight-line letter; head and body letter (ascender) (l).
Vocabulary on page: leg, lion, lazy.
Extra vocabulary: lot, love, little, like, light.

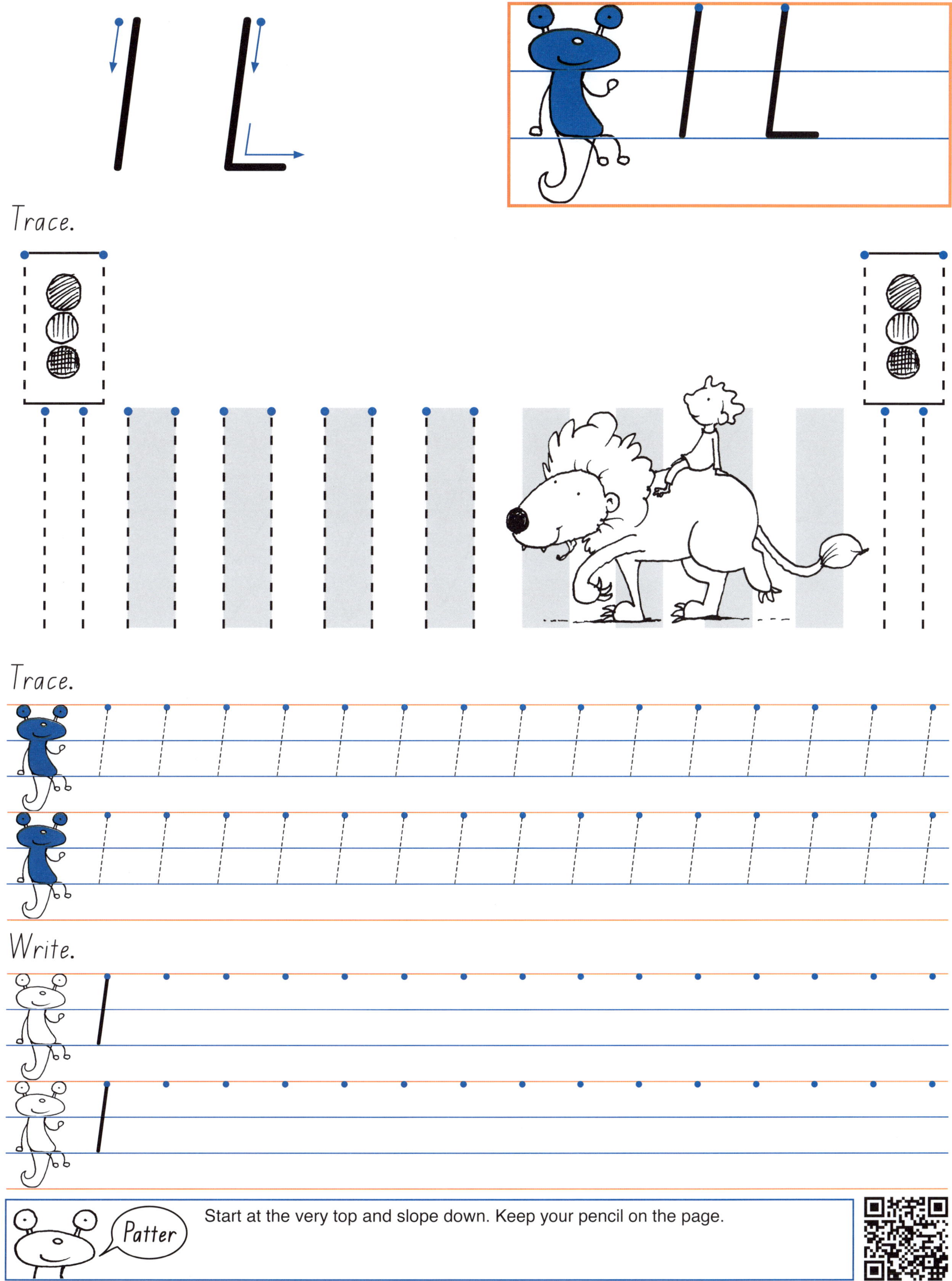
Trace.
Trace.
Write.
Patter
Start at the very top and slope down. Keep your pencil on the page.

Chant:

foxy ox

x x x

Track the pattern.

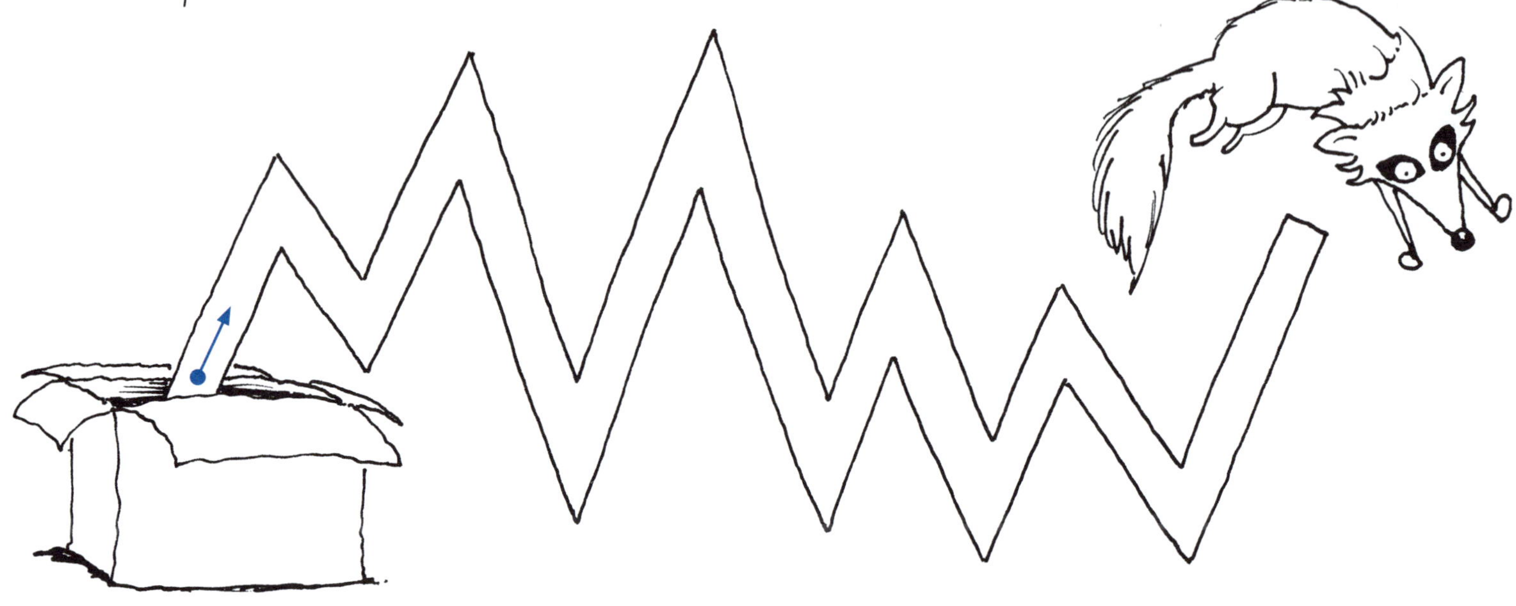

Trace the pattern. Find and write x.

Track.

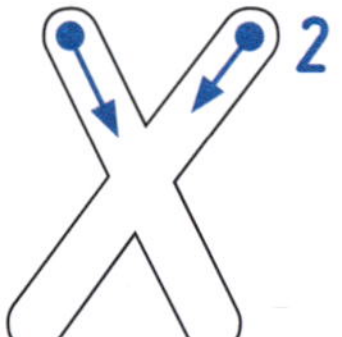 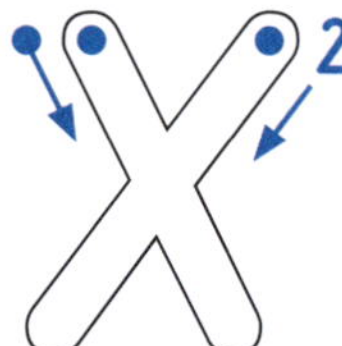 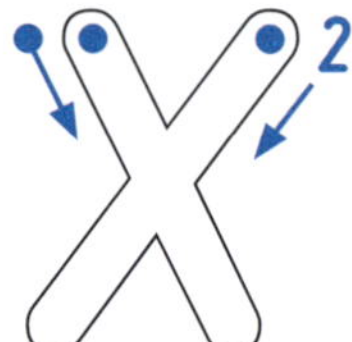 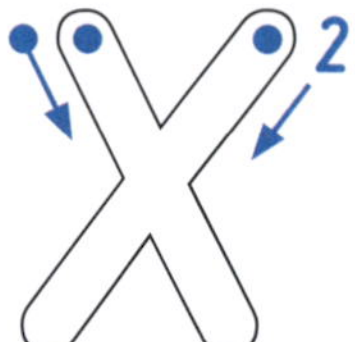 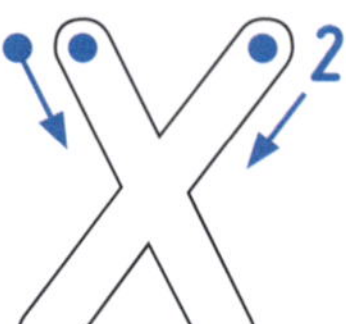 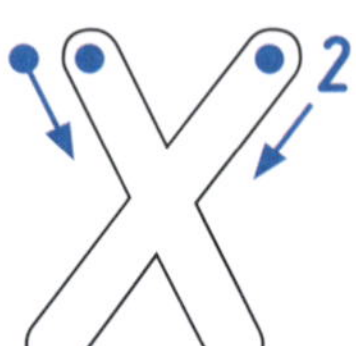

Handwriting: straight-line letter; body letter (x).
Vocabulary on page: ox, box, fox, foxy.
Extra vocabulary: x-ray.

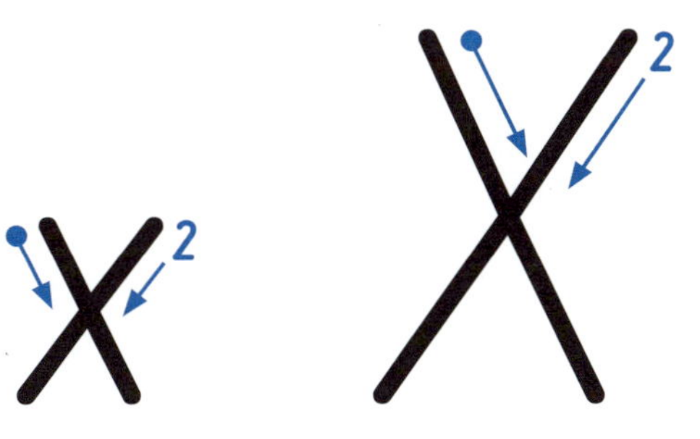

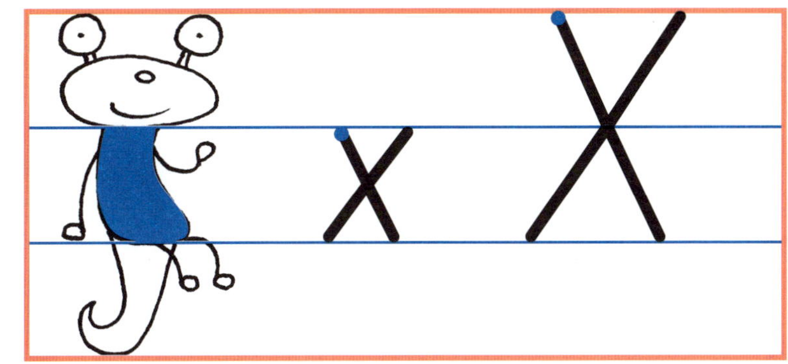

Track.

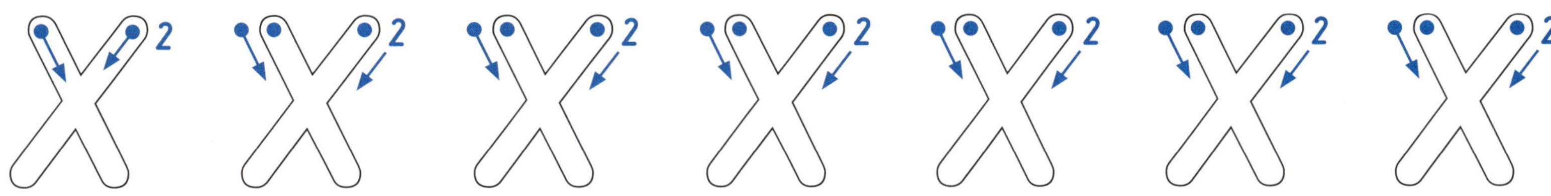

Trace.

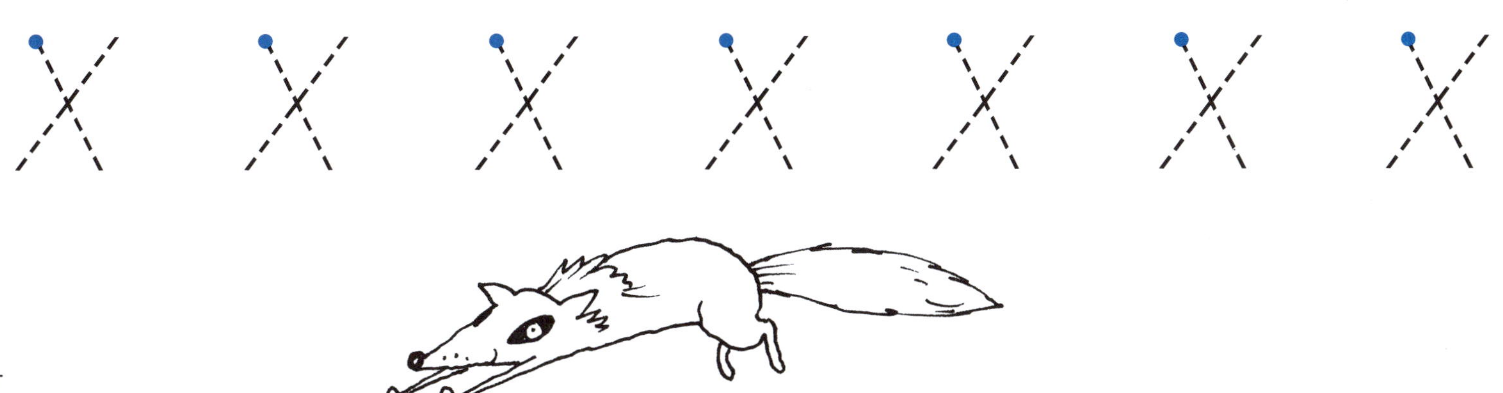

Trace.

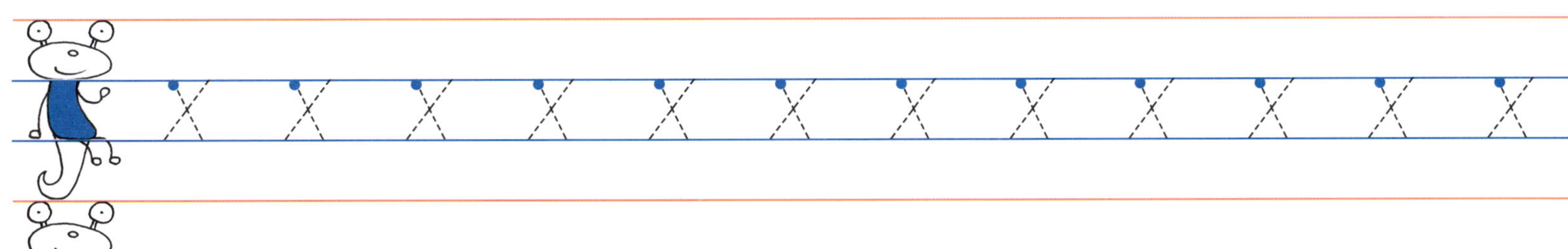

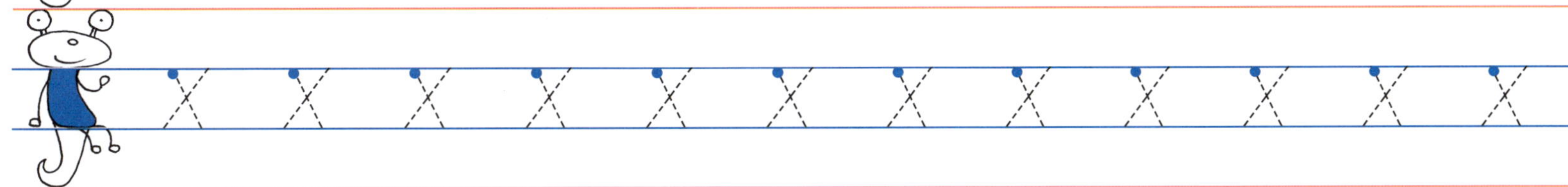

Write.

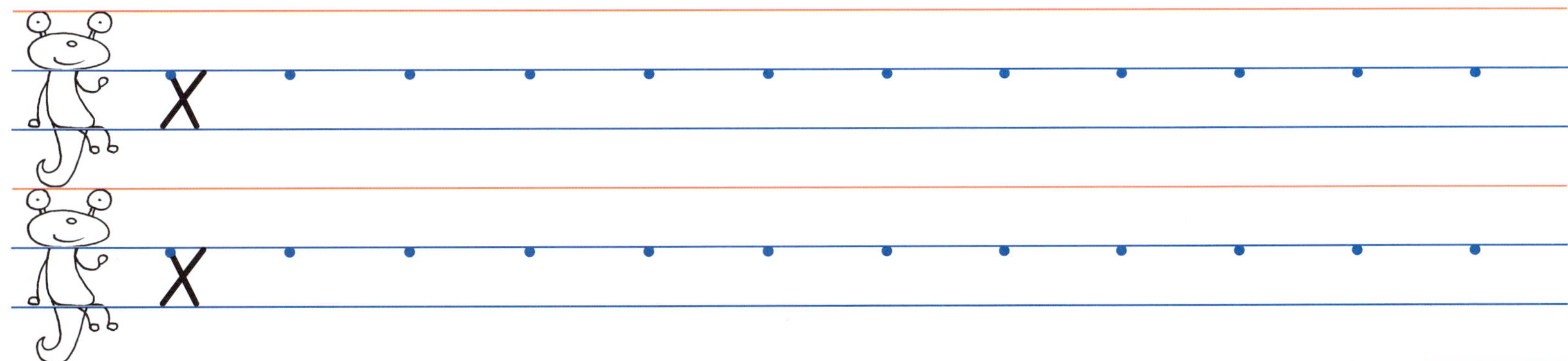

Make a straight stroke. Lift your pencil and cross it with another straight stroke.

Chant:

zigzag zebra
z z z

Trace the pattern.

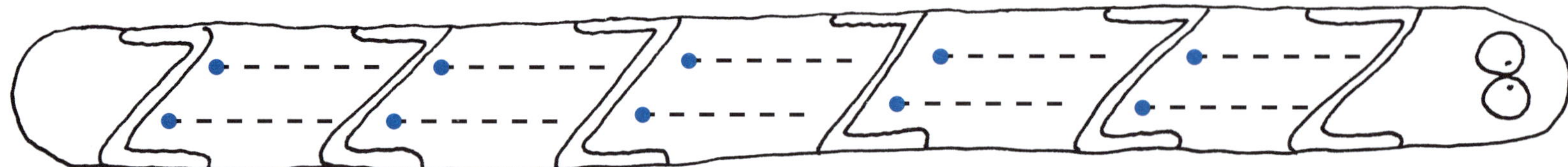

Trace the pattern.

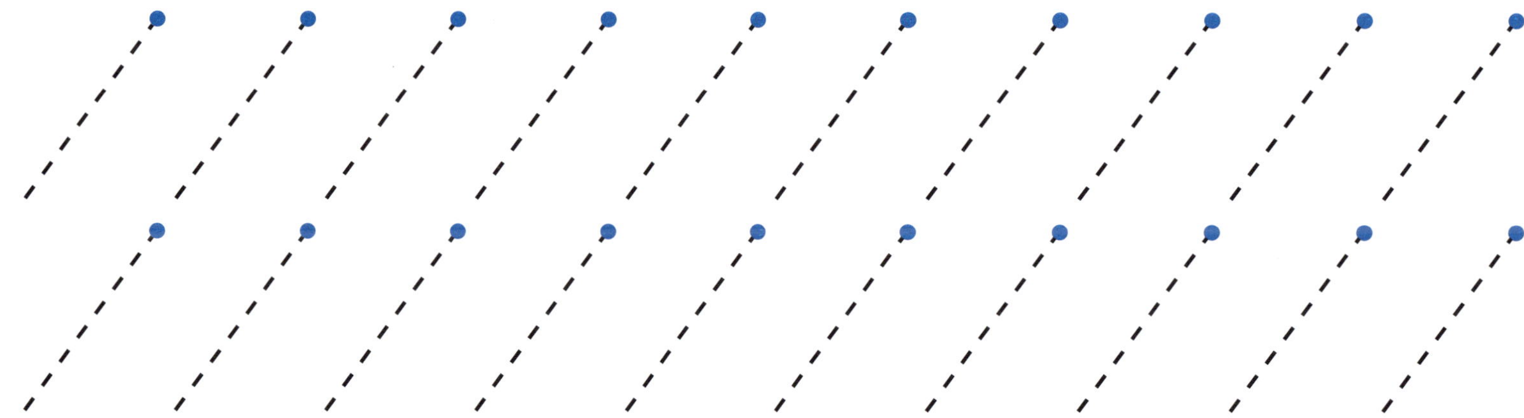

Find z.

Track.

Handwriting: straight-line letter; body letter (z).
Vocabulary on page: zebra, zigzag.
Extra vocabulary: zoo, zoom, zap, zip, zipper, jazz, pizza.

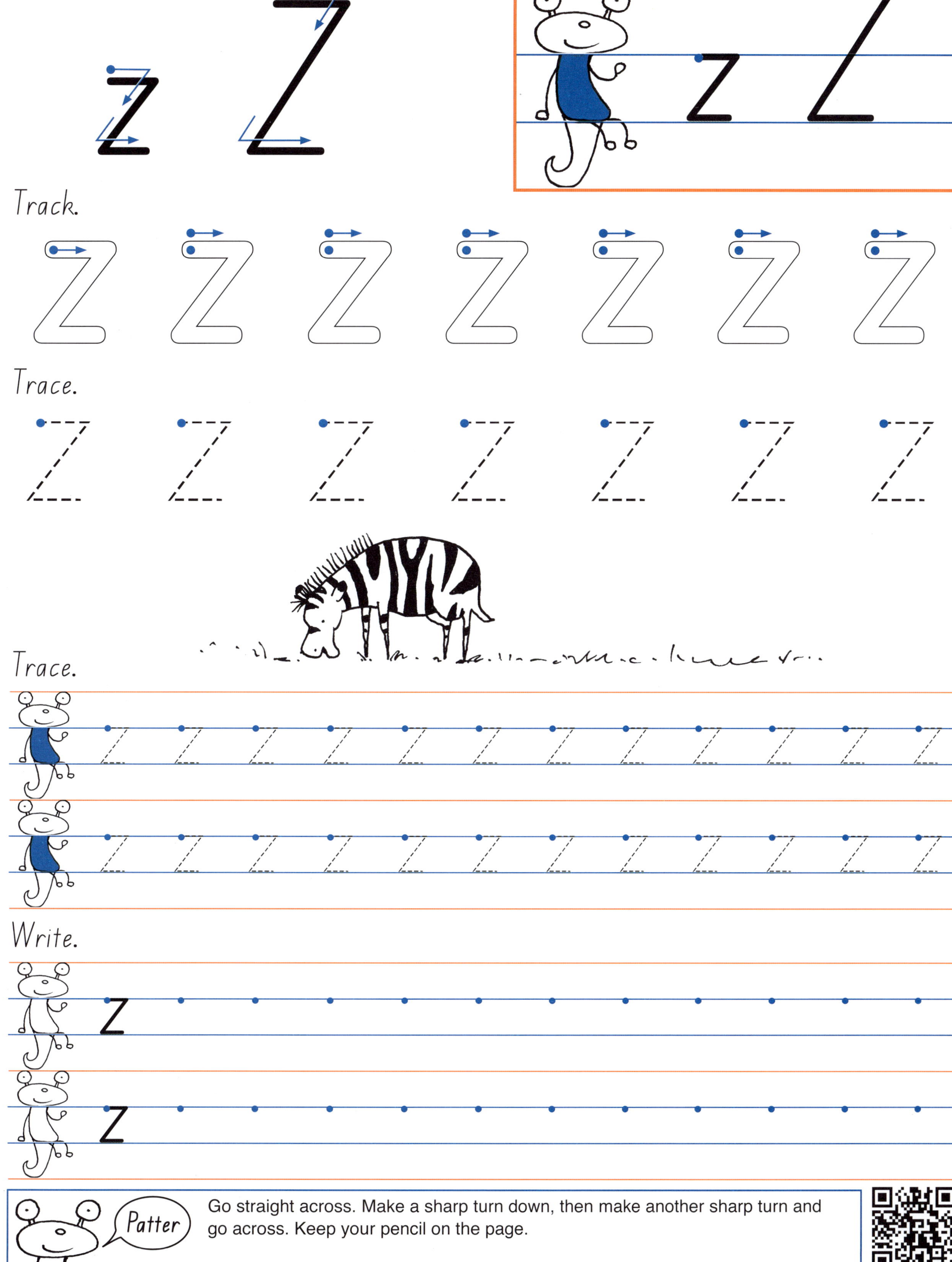
Track.
Trace.
Trace.
Write.
Patter
Go straight across. Make a sharp turn down, then make another sharp turn and go across. Keep your pencil on the page.

Chant:

ugly undies
u u u

Trace the pattern.

Find u.

u

Trace the pattern. Keep your pencil on the page.

Track.

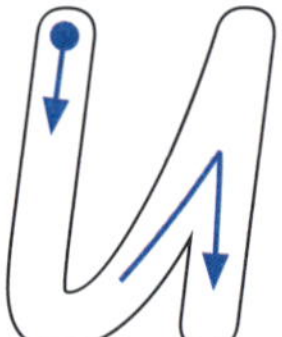  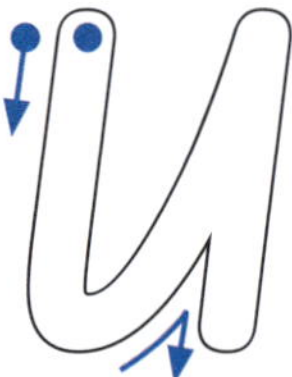 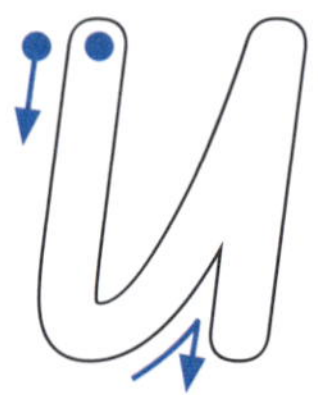  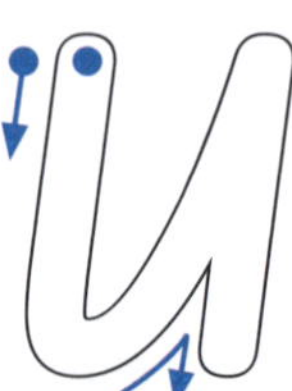

Handwriting: anticlockwise letter; body letter (u).
Vocabulary on page: ugly, undies, umbrella.
Extra vocabulary: up, under, mum, bug, but, shut, duck.

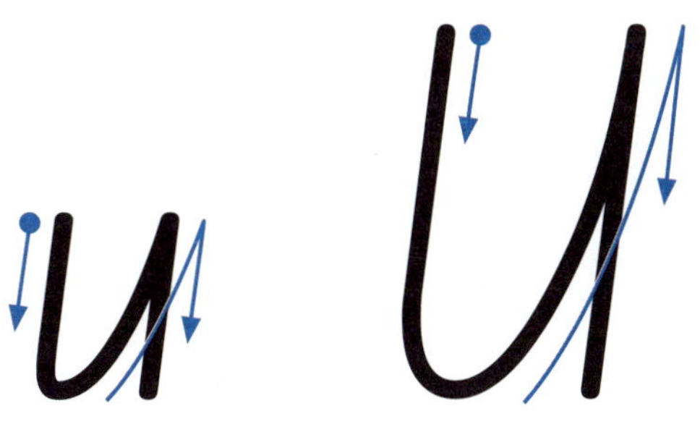

Track.

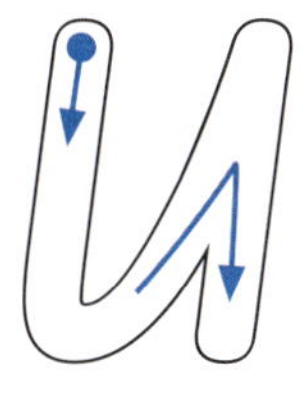  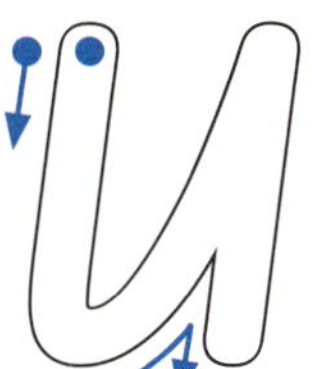 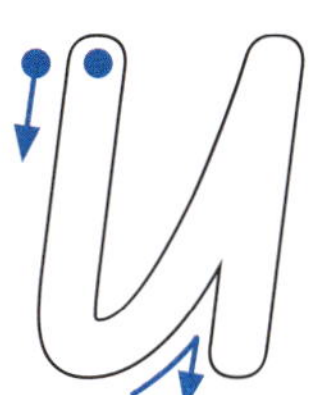  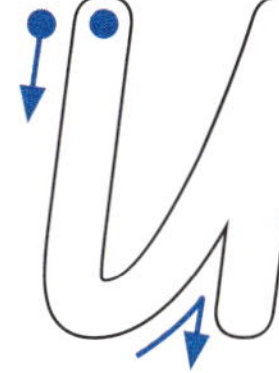

Trace.

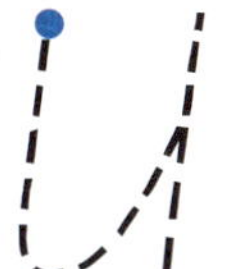   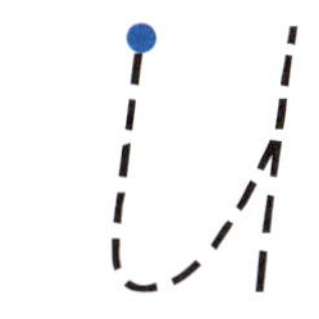   

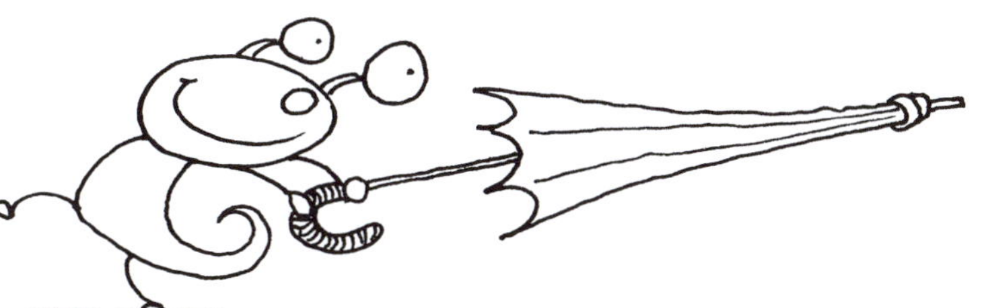

Trace.

 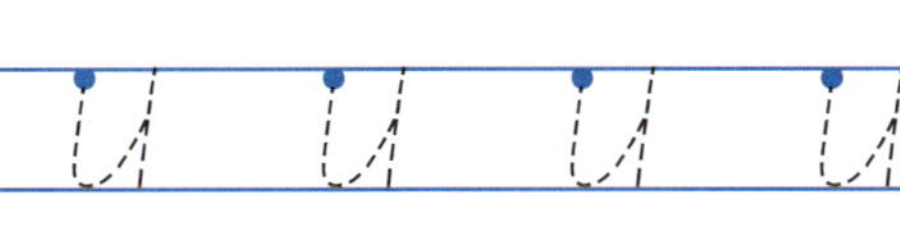 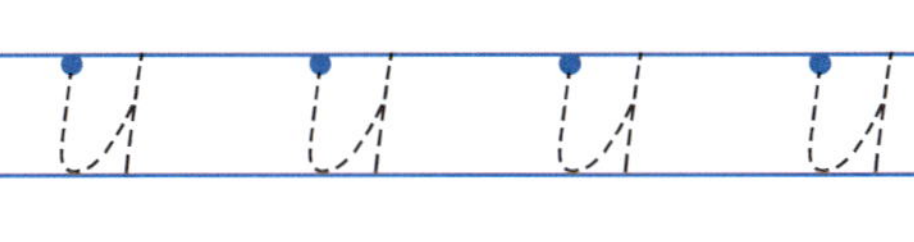 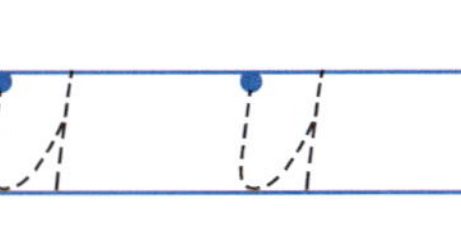 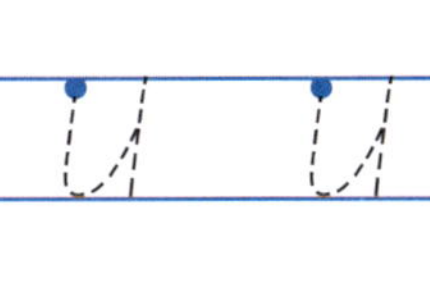 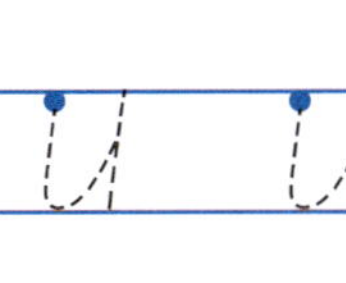 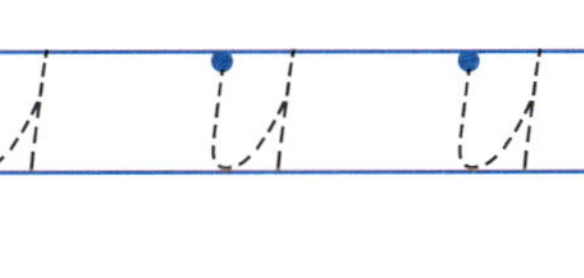

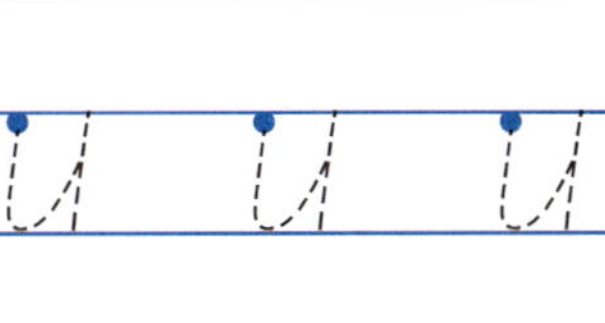

Write.

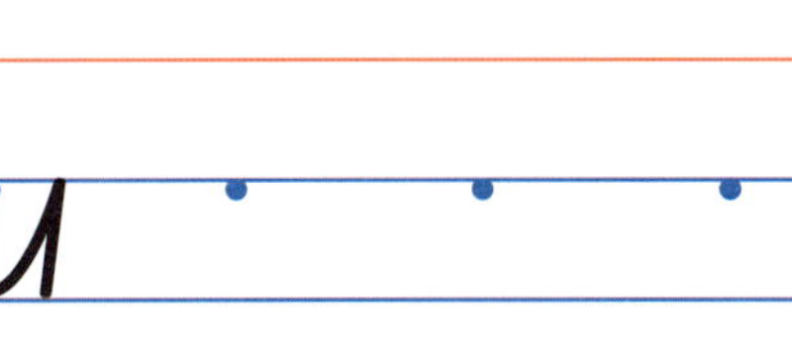

Go down, around, up and down. Keep your pencil on the page.

Chant:

vicious vulture

v v v

Trace the pattern.

Trace the pattern. Keep your pencil on the page.

Trace the pattern. Turn each pattern into a picture.

Track.

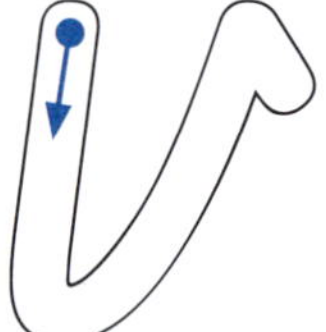

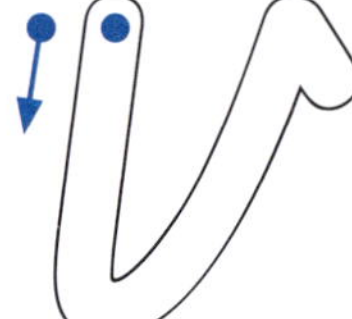

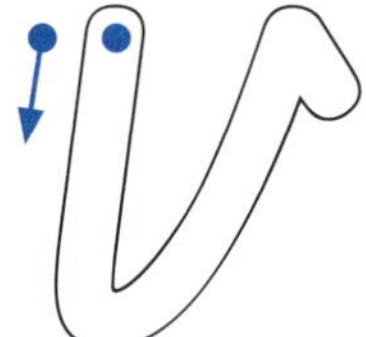

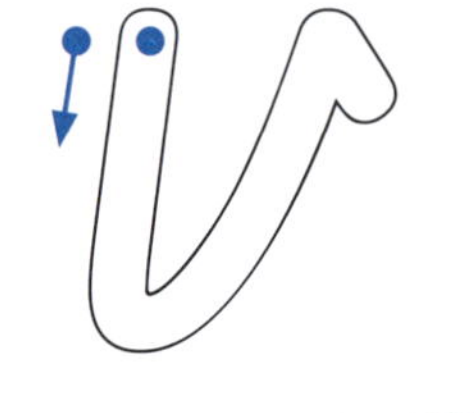

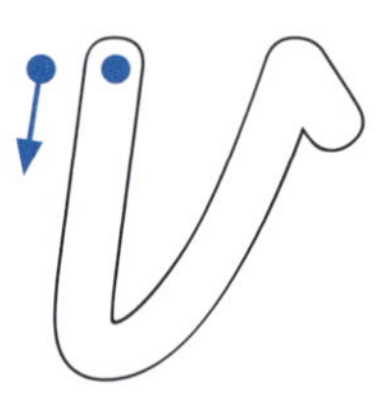

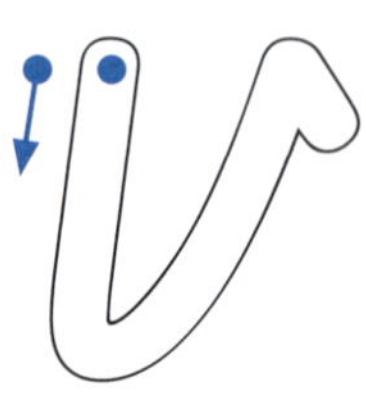

Handwriting: anticlockwise letter; body letter (v).
Vocabulary on page: violin, vulture, vicious.
Extra vocabulary: vet, van, very.

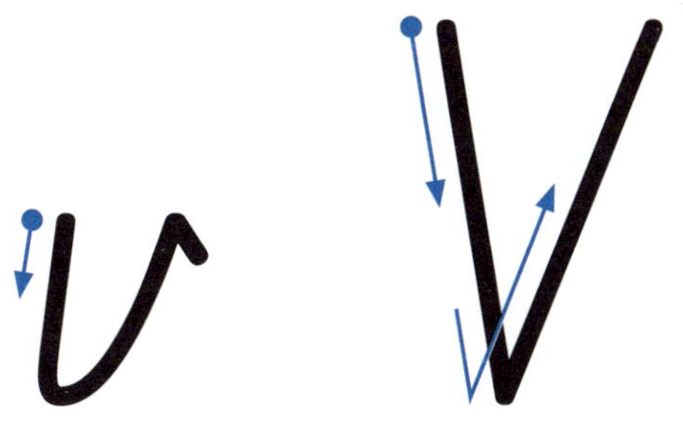

Track.

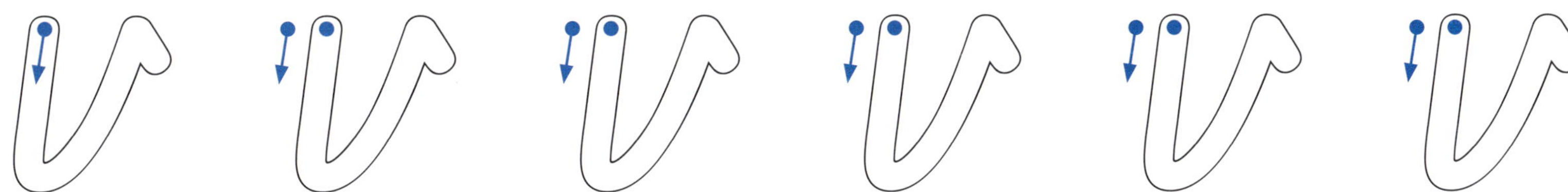

Trace.

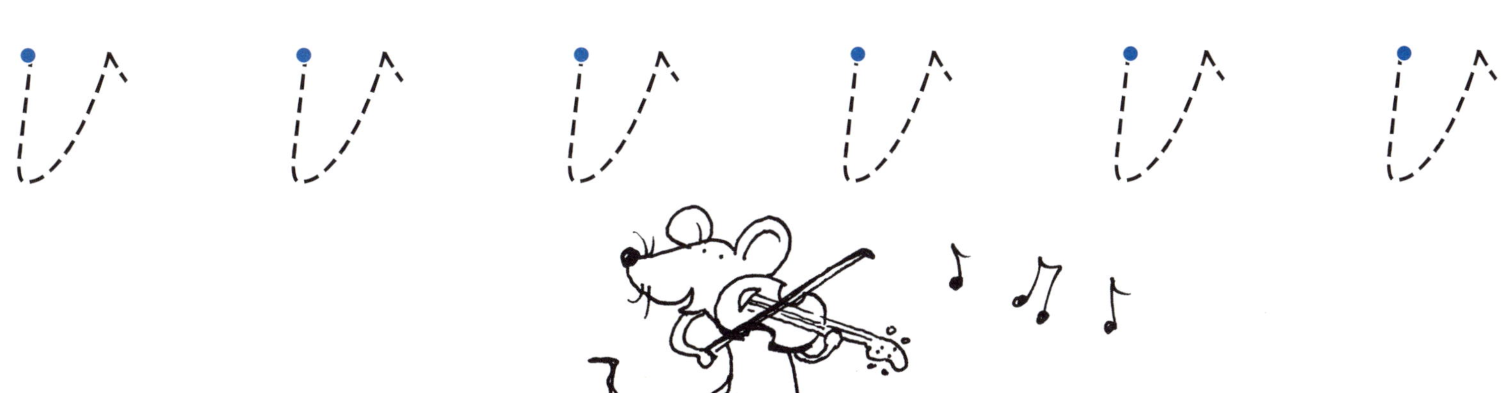

Trace.

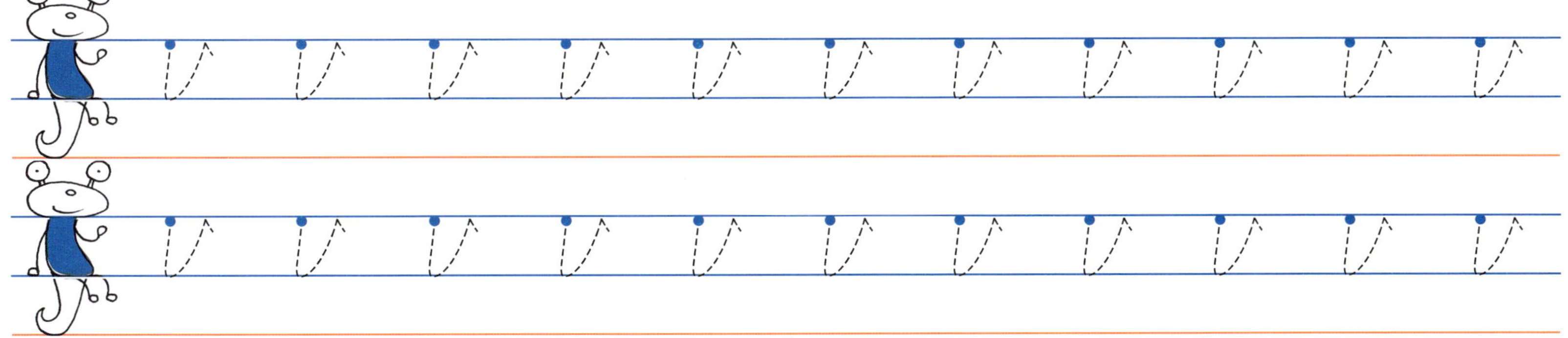

Write.

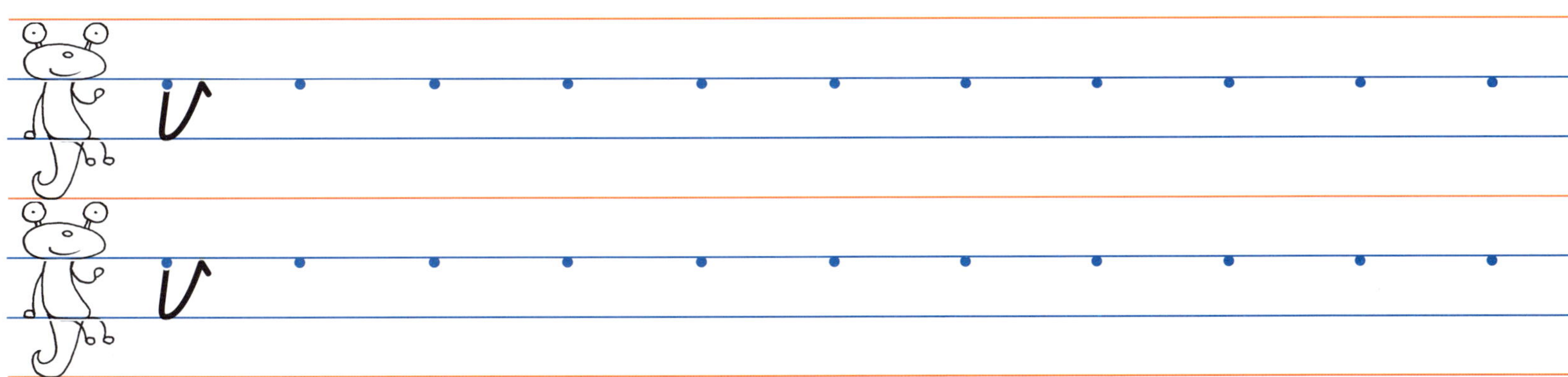

Go down, around and up, then exit with a short stroke. Keep your pencil on the page.

Chant:

wiggly wolf

w w w

Trace the pattern.

Trace the pattern. Keep your pencil on the page.

Trace the pattern. Turn each pattern into a picture.

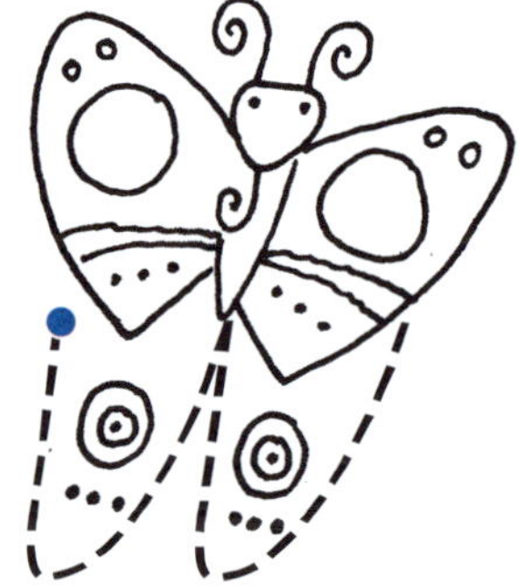

Track.

Handwriting: anticlockwise letter; body letter (w).
Vocabulary on page: wiggly, wings, wolf, whale.
Extra vocabulary: wet, win, we, wish, when, where, why.

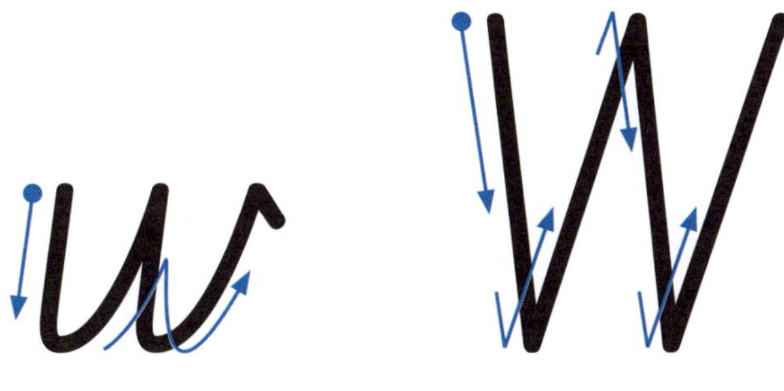

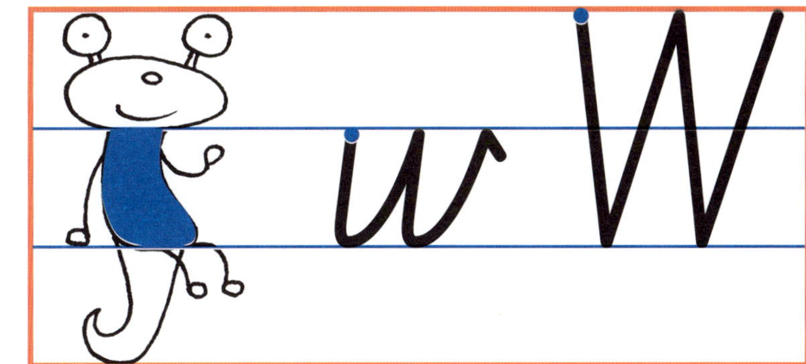

Track.

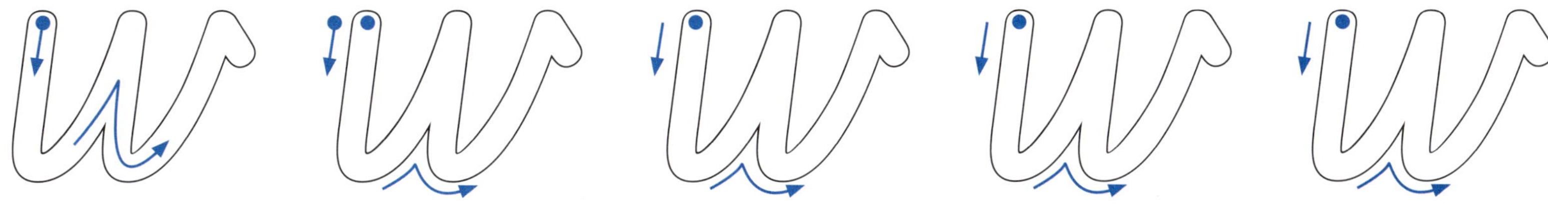

Trace.

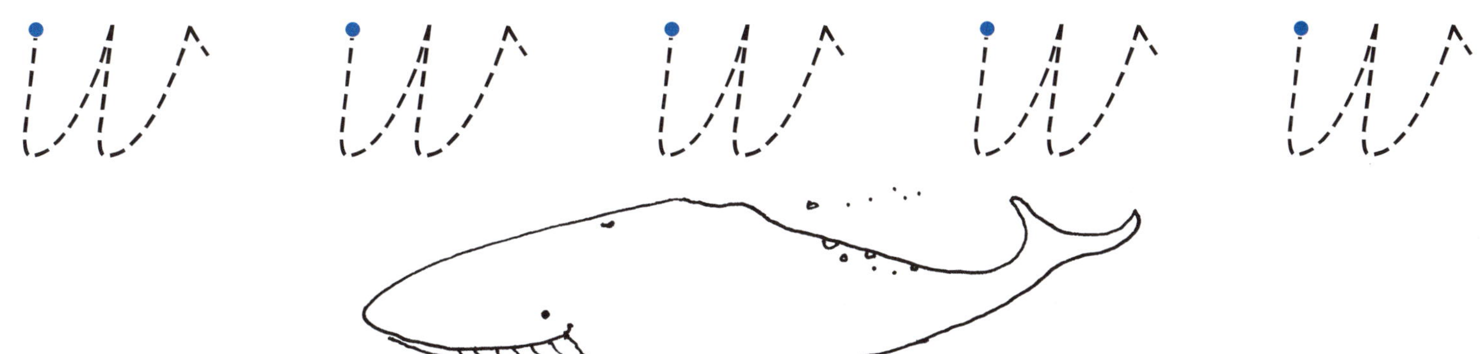

Trace.

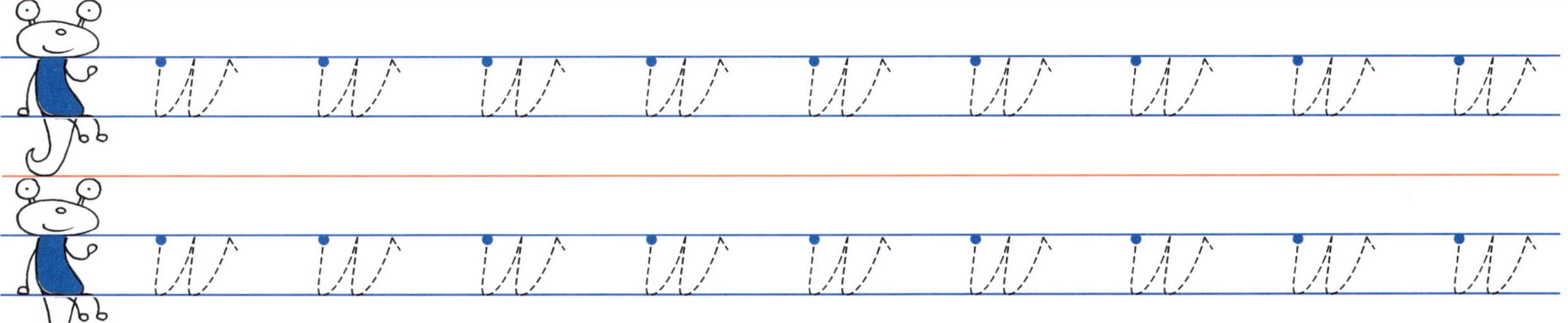

Write.

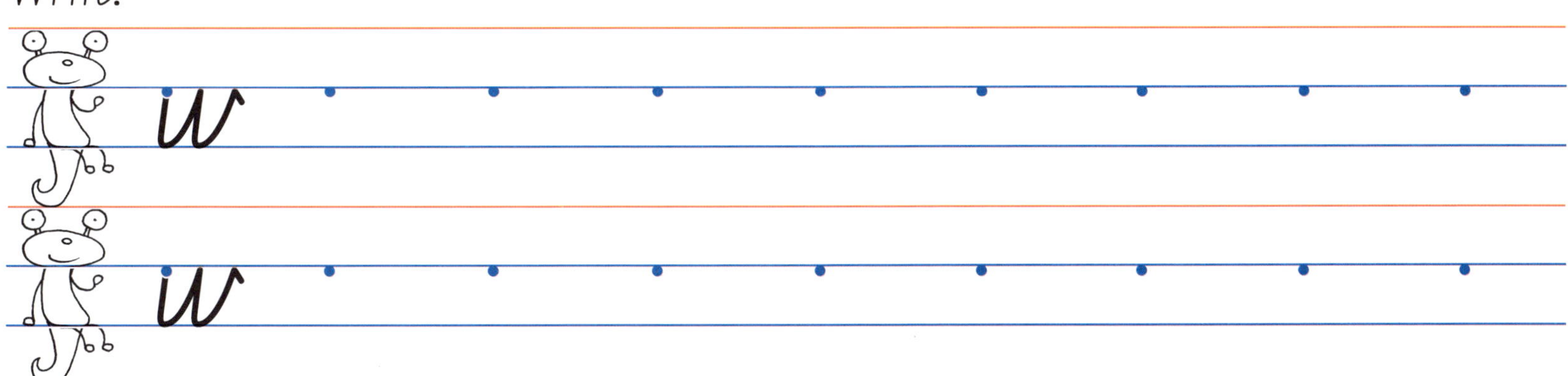

Go down, around, up then down again, around and up, then exit with a short stroke. Keep your pencil on the page.

Chant:

angry alligator

a a a

Track the pattern. Keep your pencil on the page.

Trace the pattern. Keep your pencil on the page.

Trace the pattern.

Track.

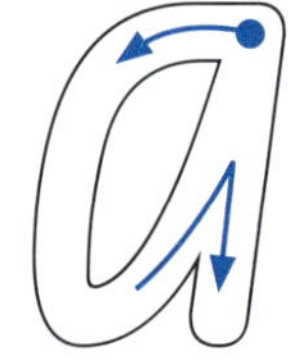  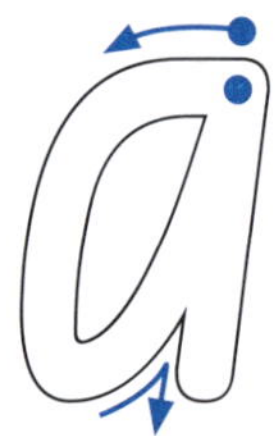 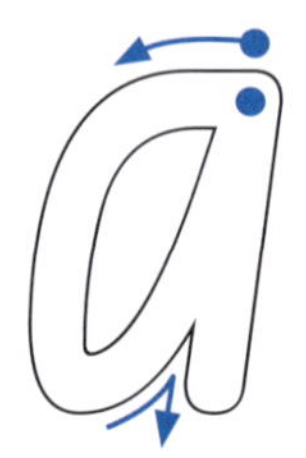 

Handwriting: anticlockwise letter; body letter (a).
Vocabulary on page: ant, anteater, angry, alligator.
Extra vocabulary: an, are, apple, cat, mat, sat, tap.

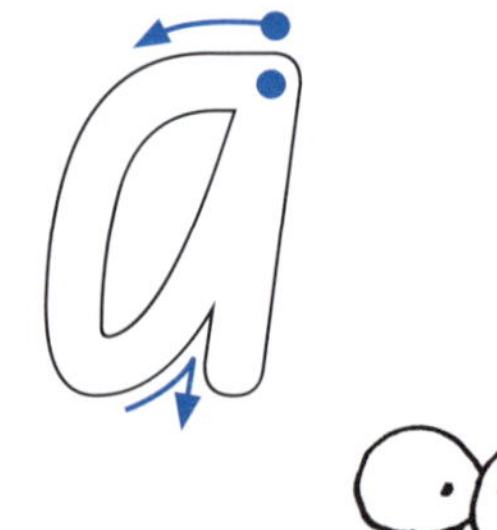

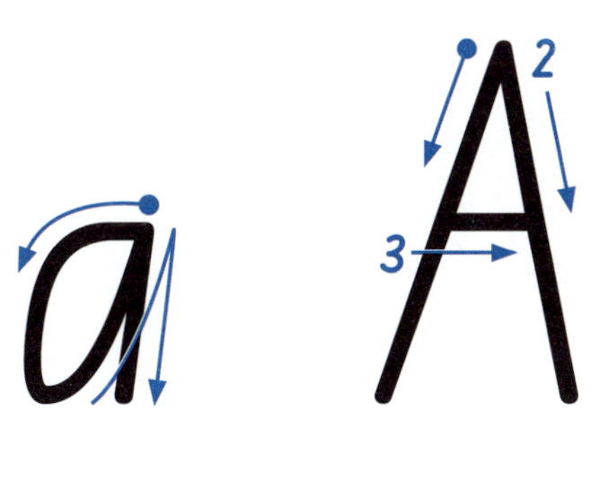

Track.

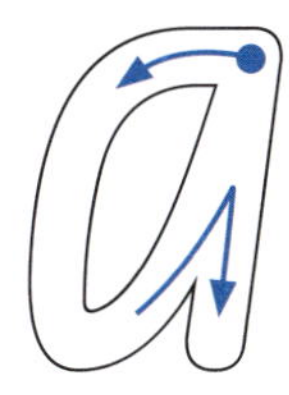      

Trace.

 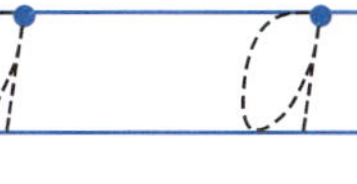 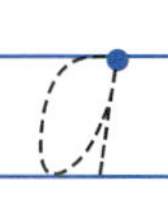 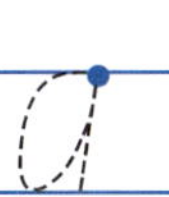 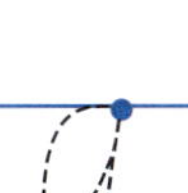  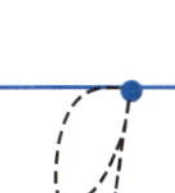 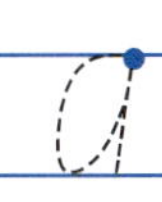 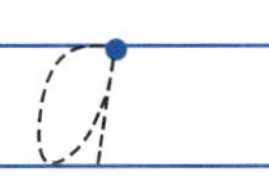

 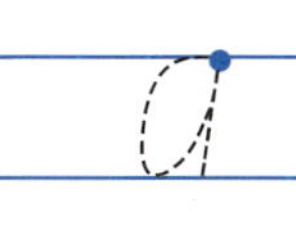 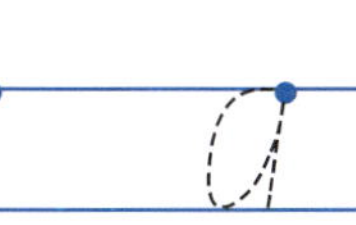  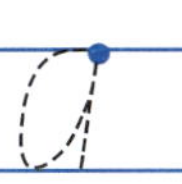 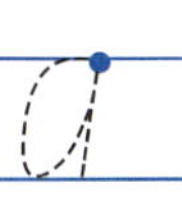 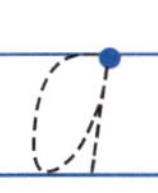 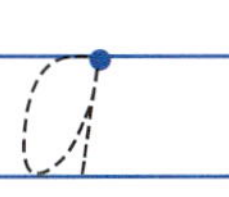 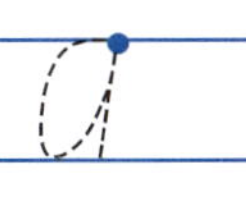

Write.

Go backwards then curve down, make a quick turn at the bottom then up to the start and drop down. Keep your pencil on the page.

Chant:

dirty dog
d d d

Trace the pattern.

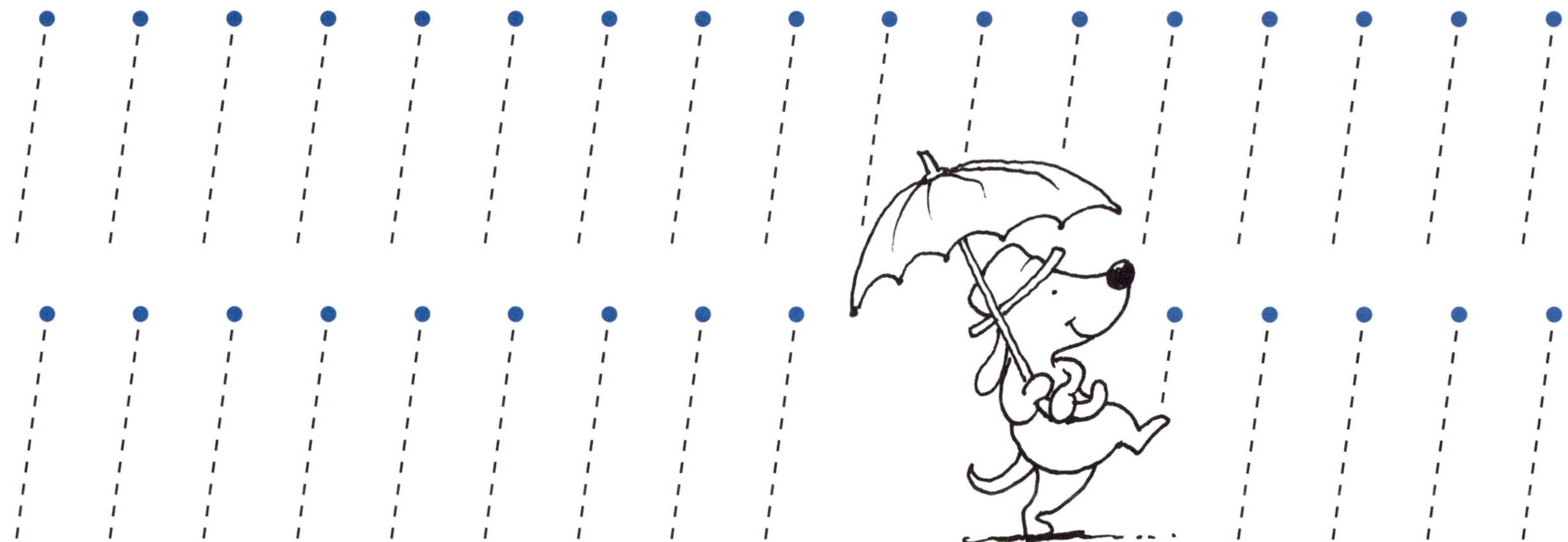

Trace the pattern.

Track.

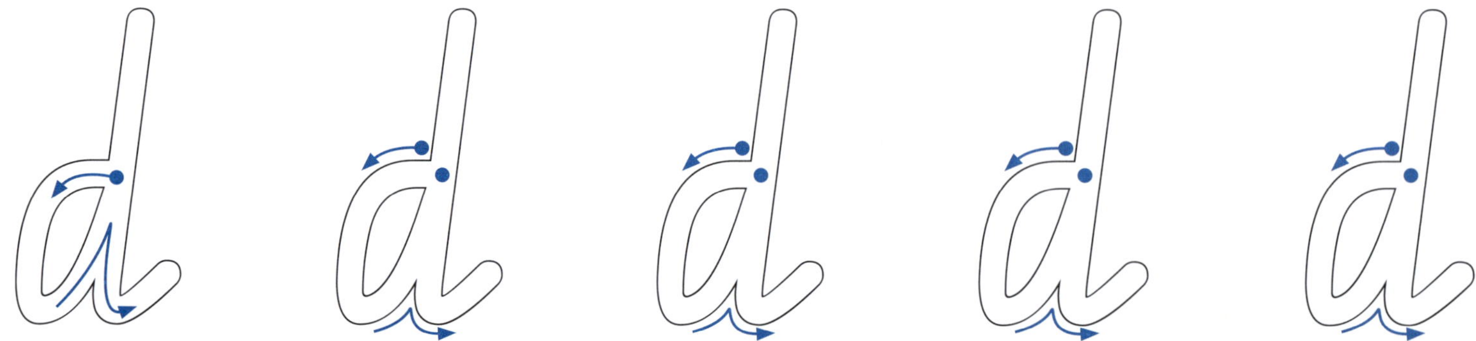

Handwriting: anticlockwise letter; head and body letter (ascender) (d).
Vocabulary on page: dog, dirty.
Extra vocabulary: do, don't, done, dip, lid, pad, down.

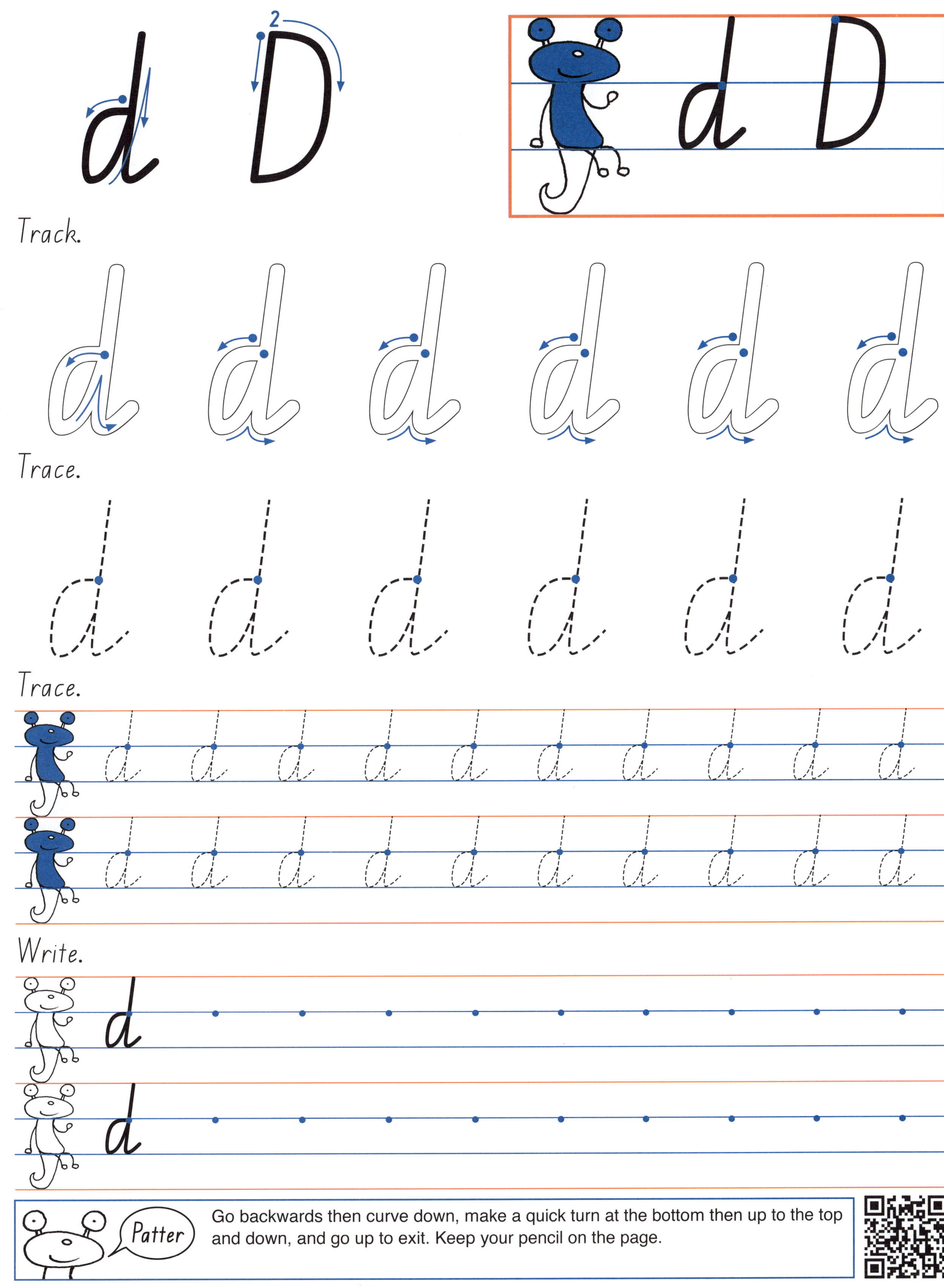

Go backwards then curve down, make a quick turn at the bottom then up to the top and down, and go up to exit. Keep your pencil on the page.

Chant:

quick quokkas

q q q

Trace the pattern. Keep your pencil on the page.

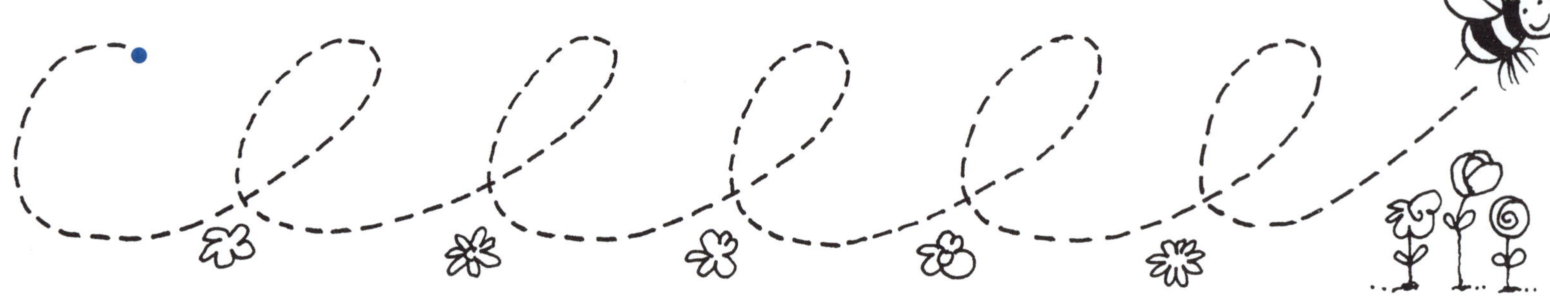

Trace the pattern. Keep your pencil on the page.

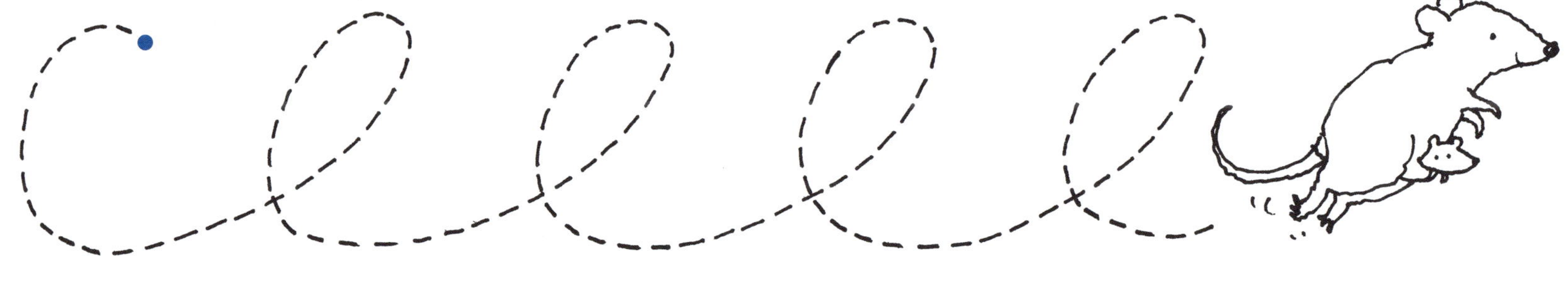

Trace.

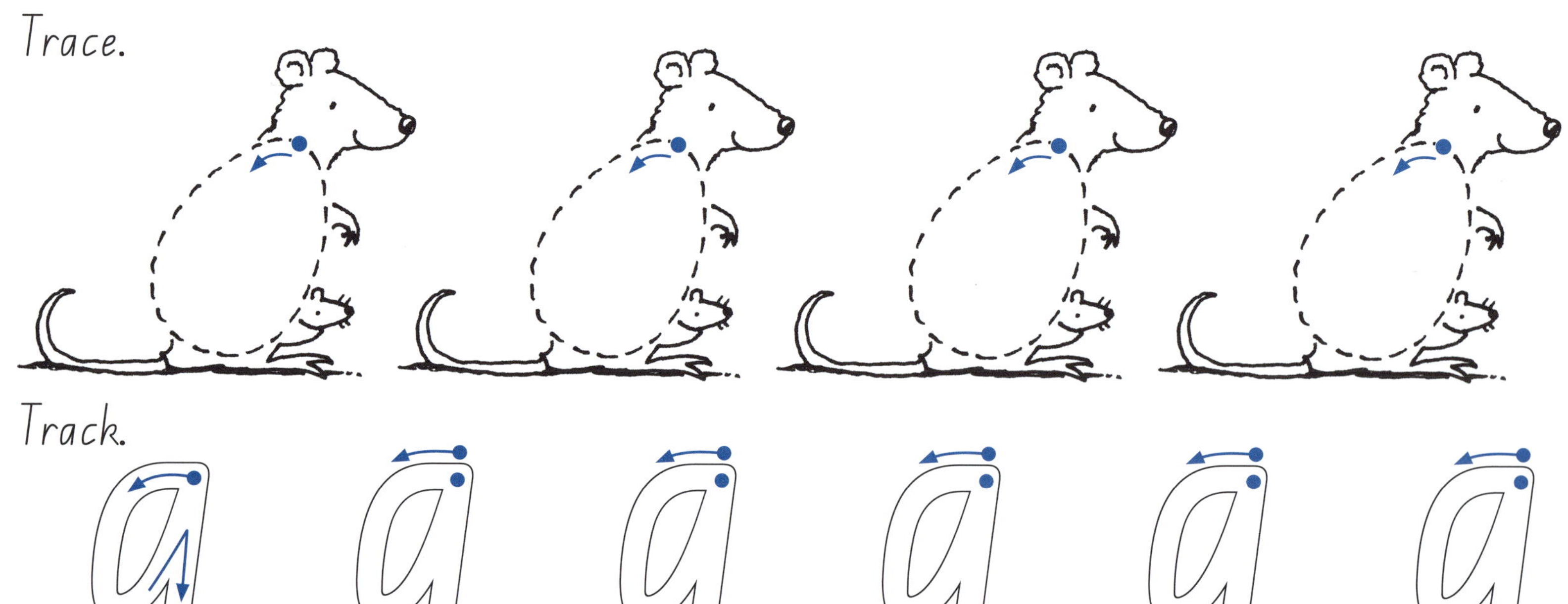

Track.

Handwriting: anticlockwise letter; body and tail letter (descender) (q).
Vocabulary on page: quick, quokka.
Extra vocabulary: quack, queen.

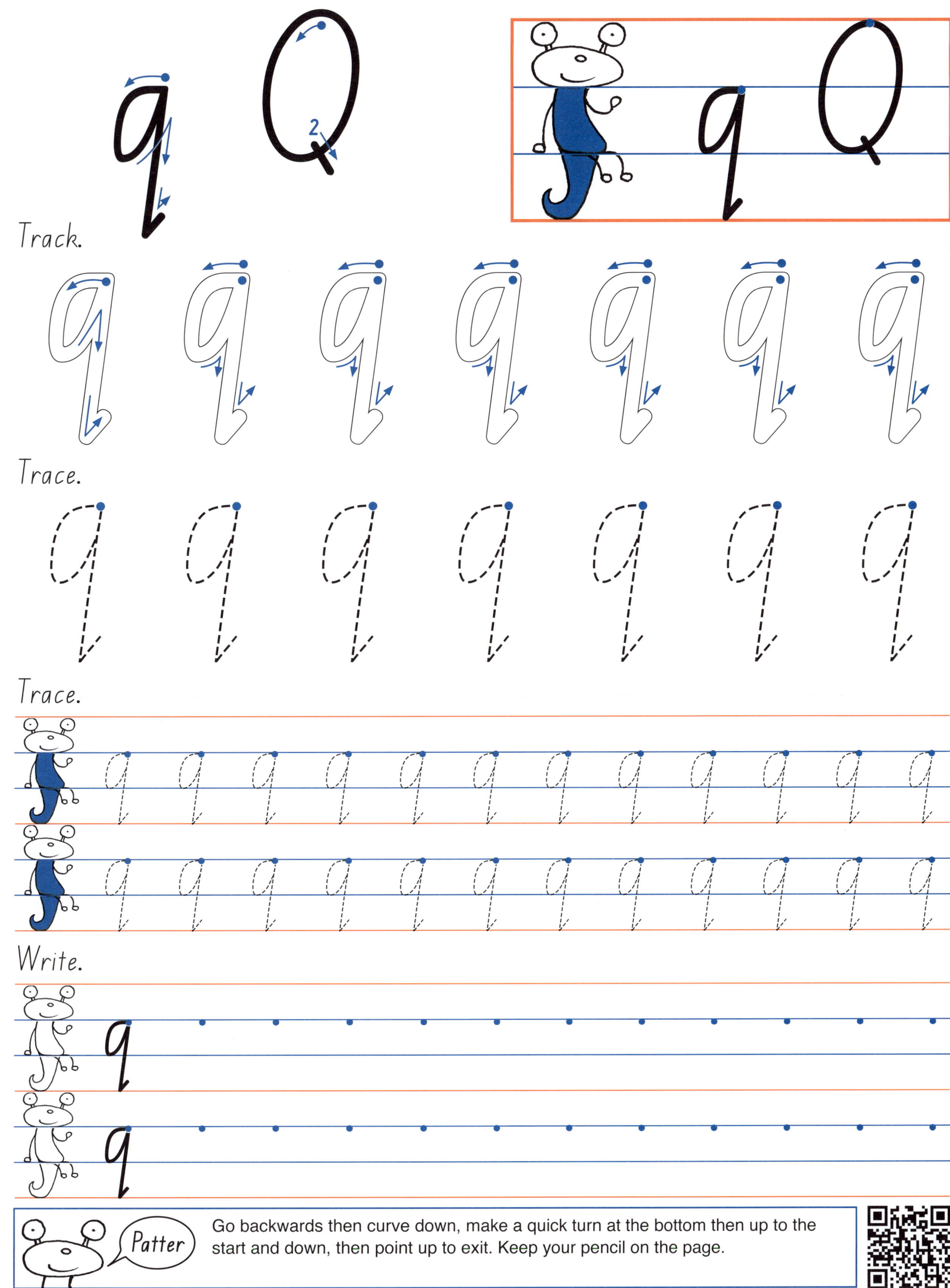

Go backwards then curve down, make a quick turn at the bottom then up to the start and down, then point up to exit. Keep your pencil on the page.

Chant:

orange octopus

o o o

Trace the pattern.

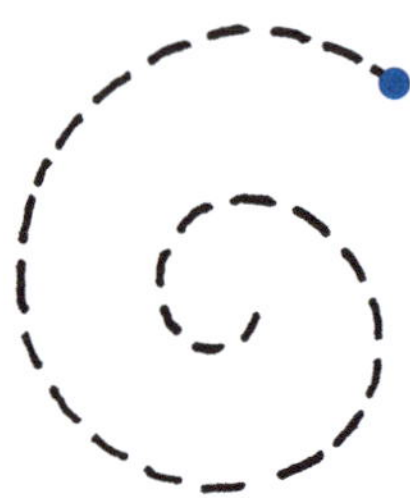  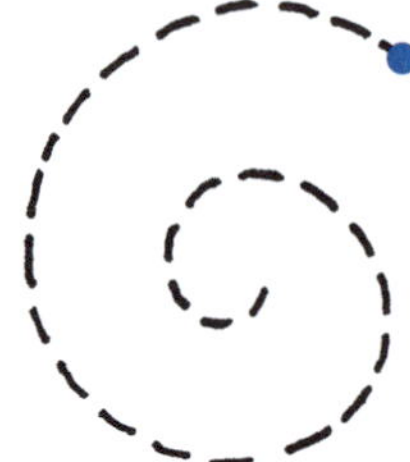  

Trace the pattern. Keep your pencil on the page.

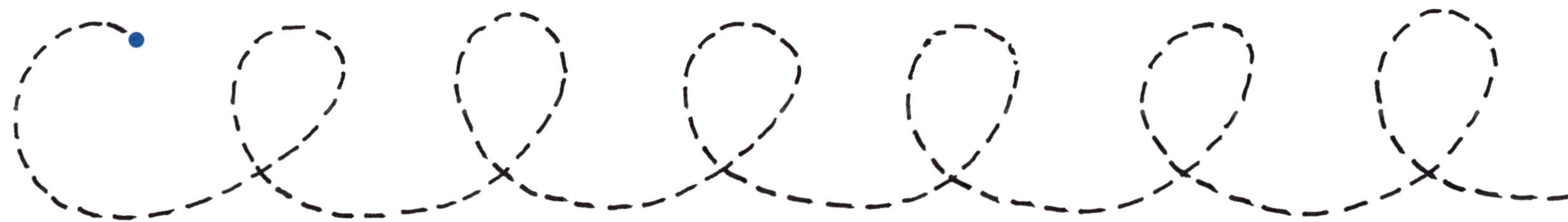

Trace the pattern.

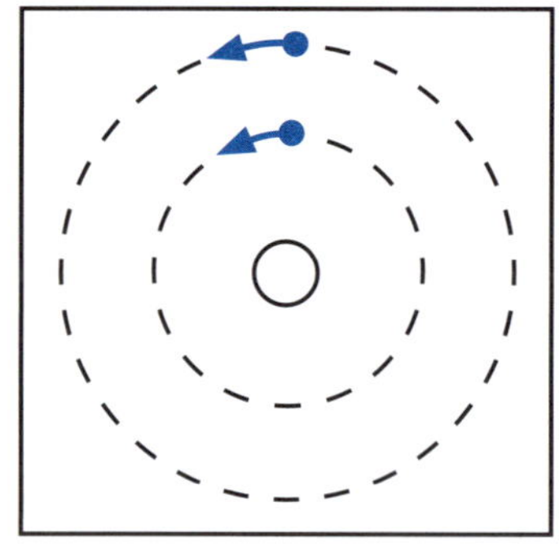 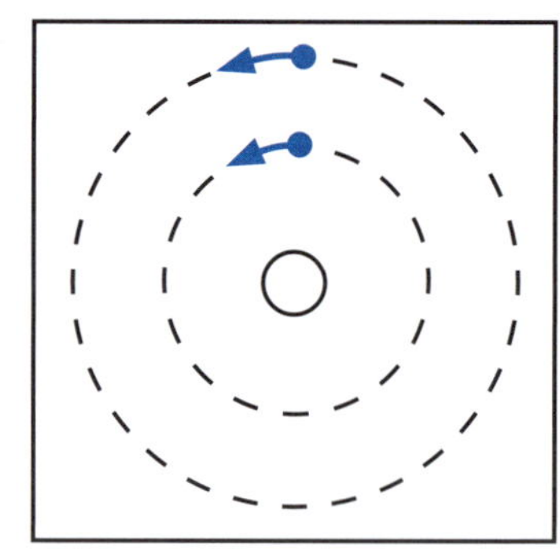 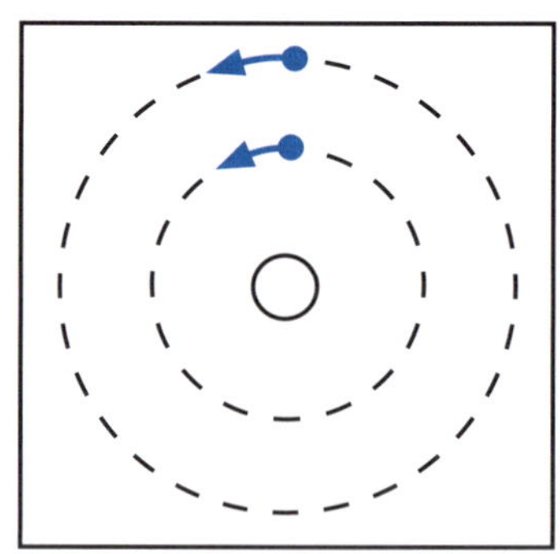 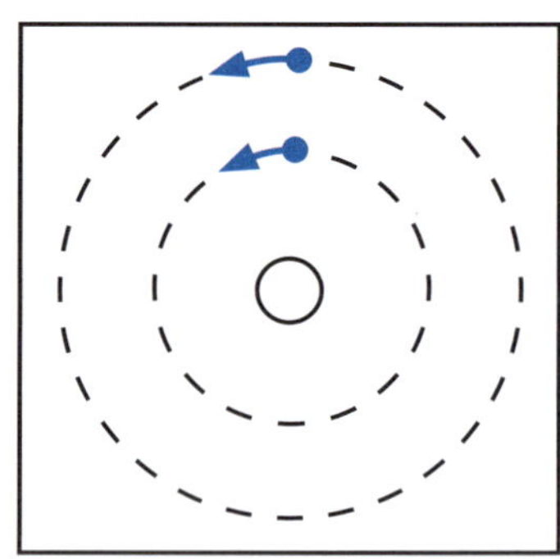

Track.

 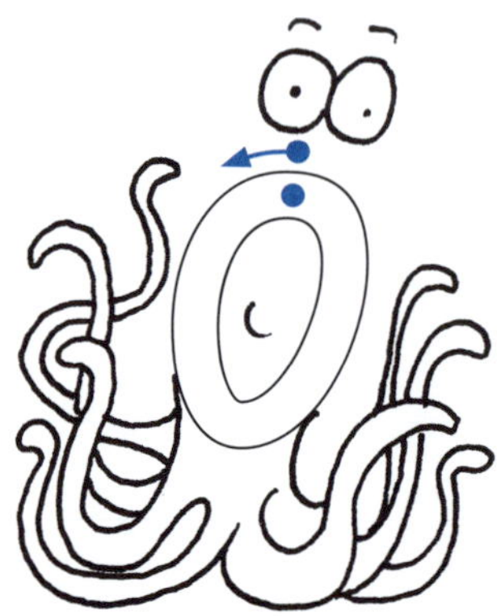  

Handwriting: anticlockwise letter; body letter (o).
Vocabulary on page: orange, octopus.
Extra vocabulary: on, not, hot, pot, of, to, log, pop, stop, go, no.

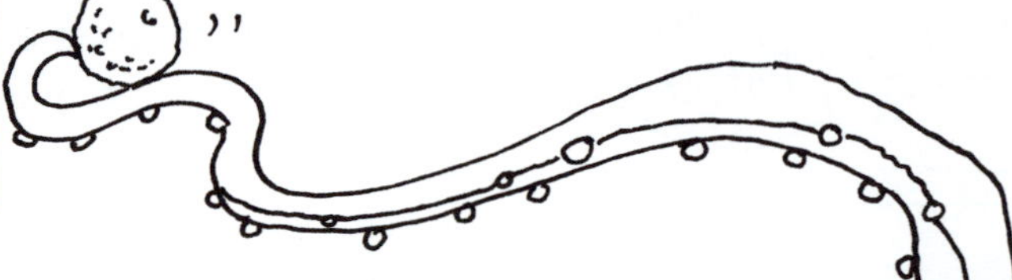

Start at 12 o'clock. Go backwards and curve down, around the bottom and up to join where you started. Keep your pencil on the page.

Chant:

energetic elephant

e e e

Trace the pattern. Keep your pencil on the page.

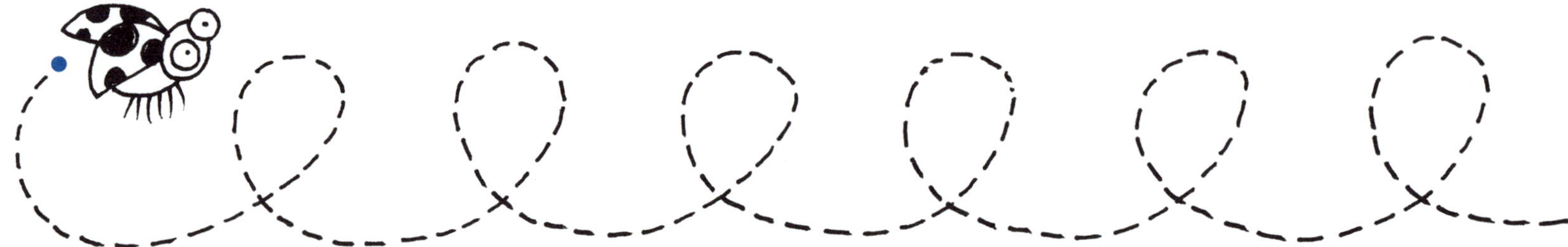

Trace the pattern.

Trace the pattern.

Track.

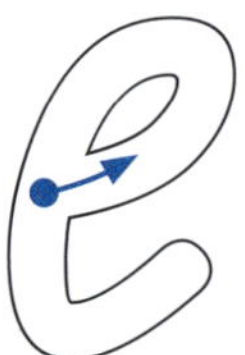

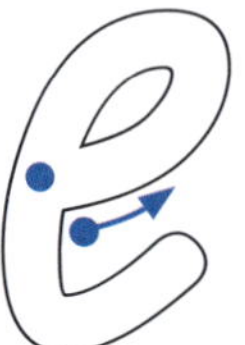

Handwriting: anticlockwise letter; body letter (e).
Vocabulary on page: egg, eagle, beetle, elephant, energetic.
Extra vocabulary: eat, he, she, the, red, net, yell, men.

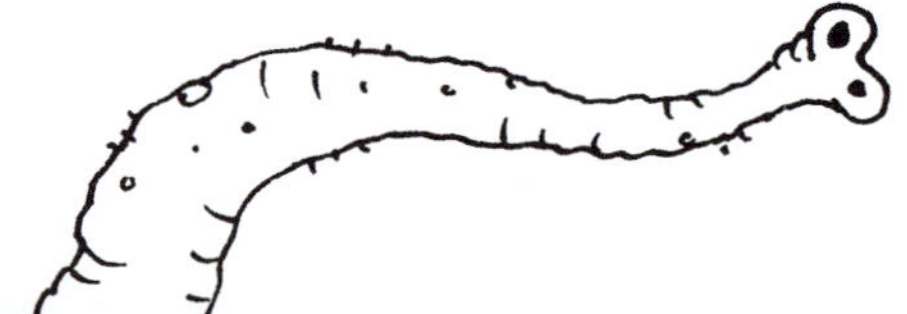

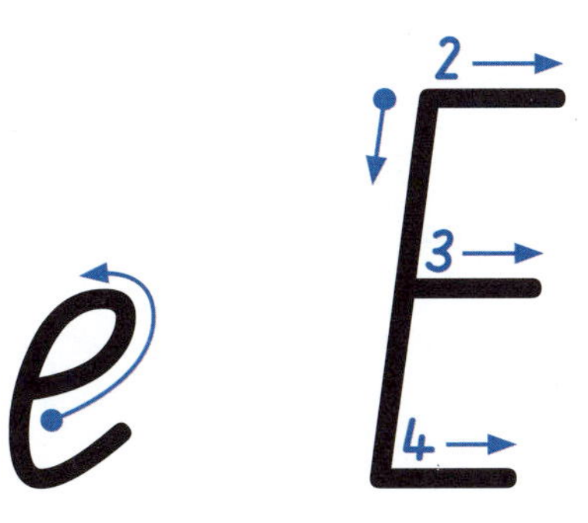

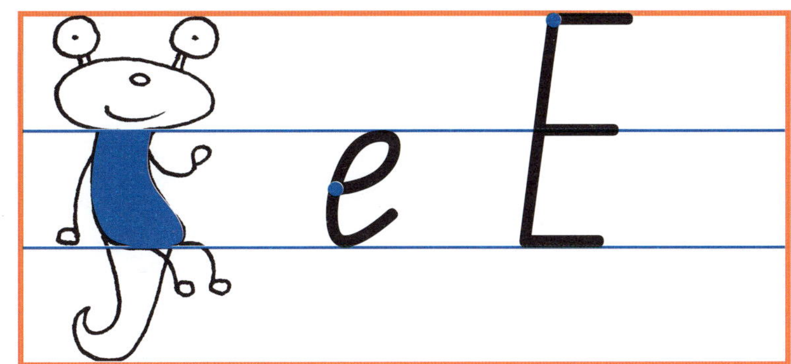

Track.

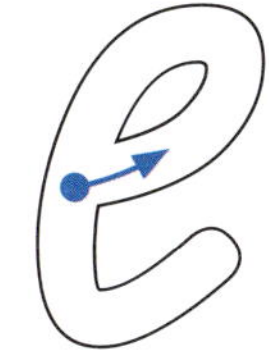 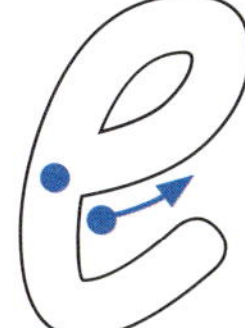 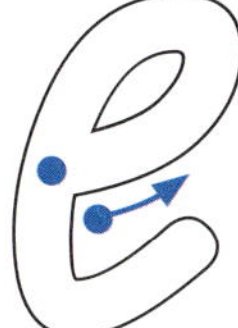 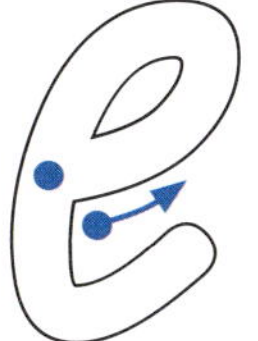 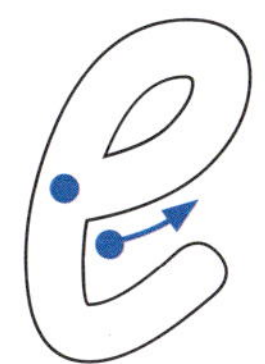 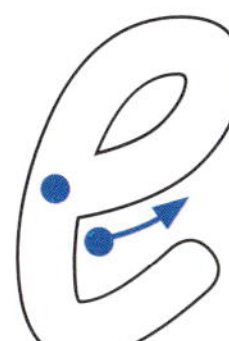 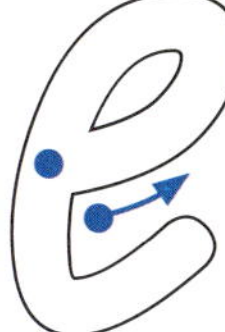

Trace.

   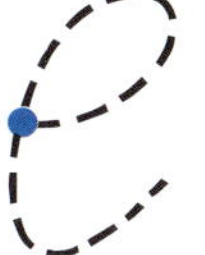 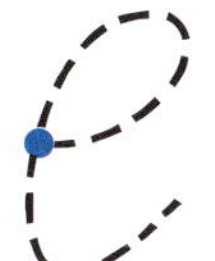  

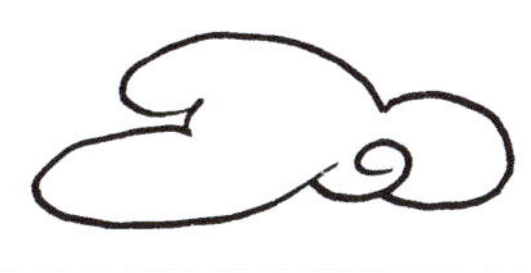   

Trace.

   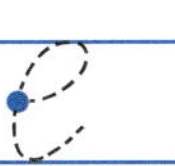 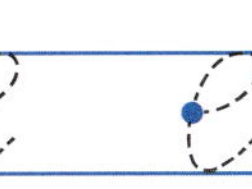 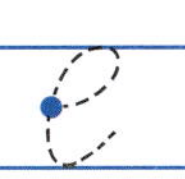 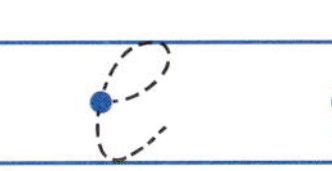 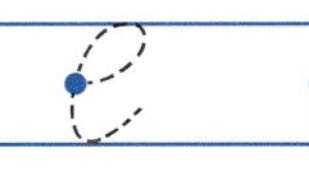

 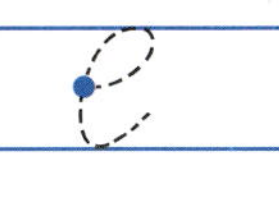 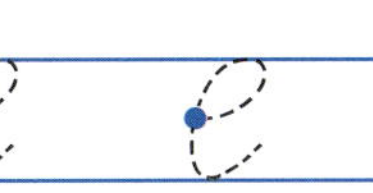   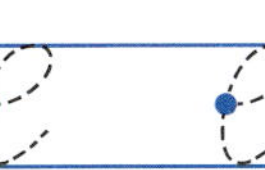 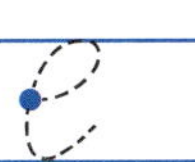 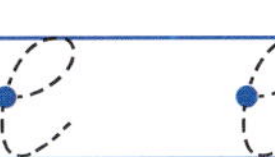 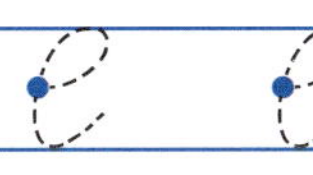

Write.

   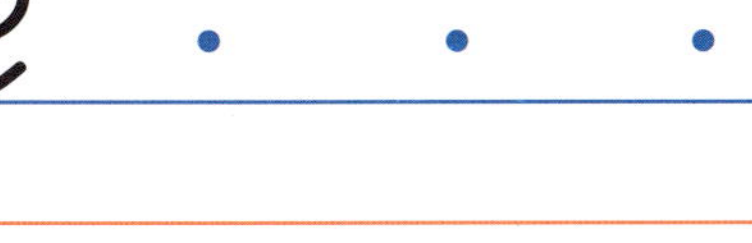 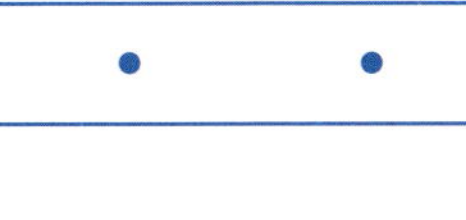 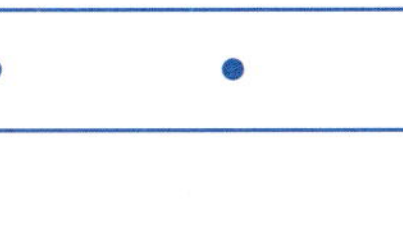 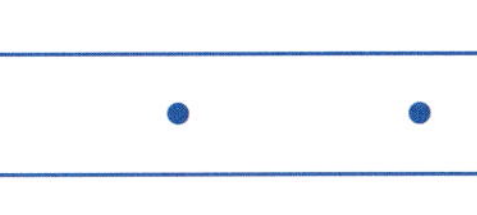

  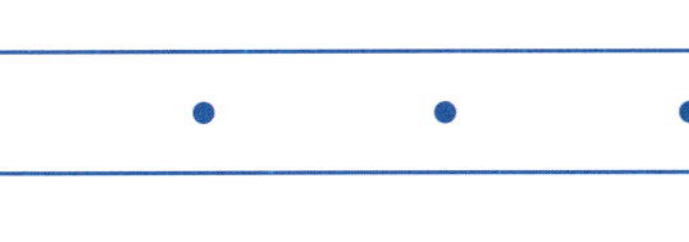

Start in the middle, sweep up and make a smooth turn. Go around to end. Keep your pencil on the page.

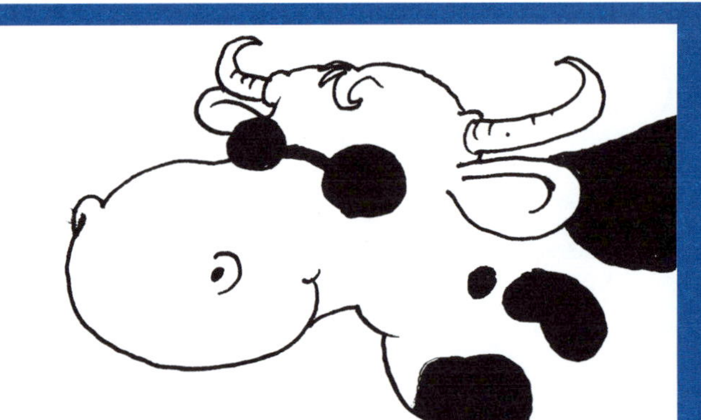

Chant:

cool cow

c c c

Trace the pattern.

Find c.

Track.

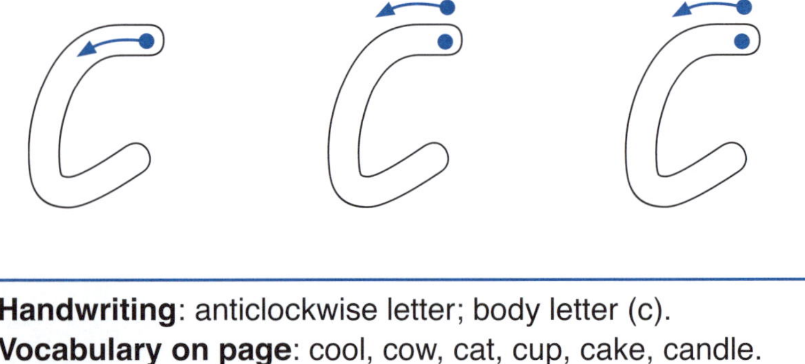

Handwriting: anticlockwise letter; body letter (c).
Vocabulary on page: cool, cow, cat, cup, cake, candle.
Extra vocabulary: cold.

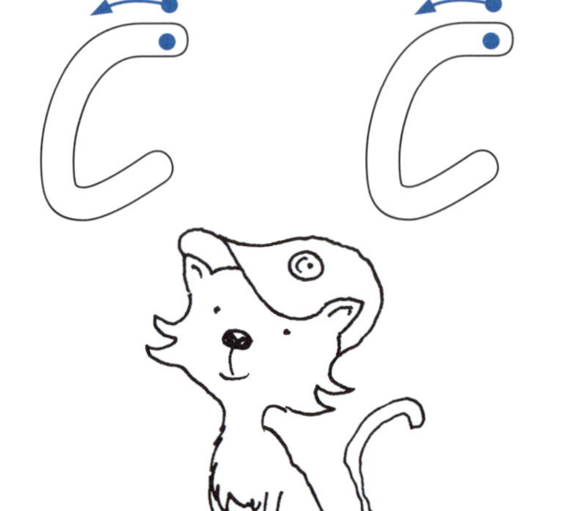

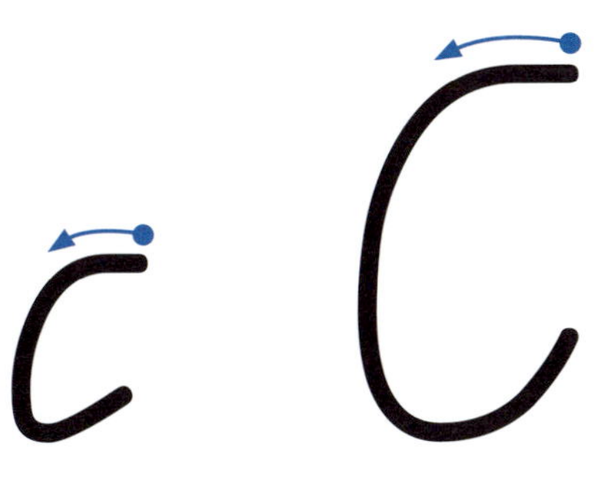
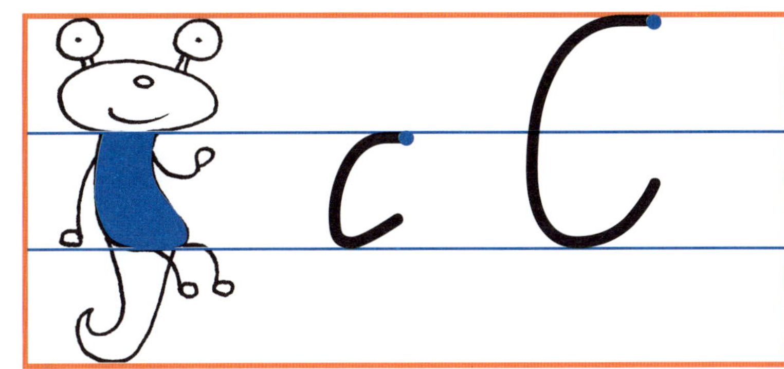

Track.

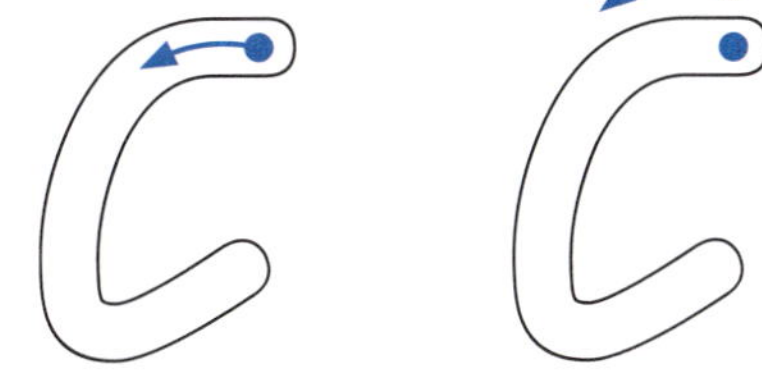
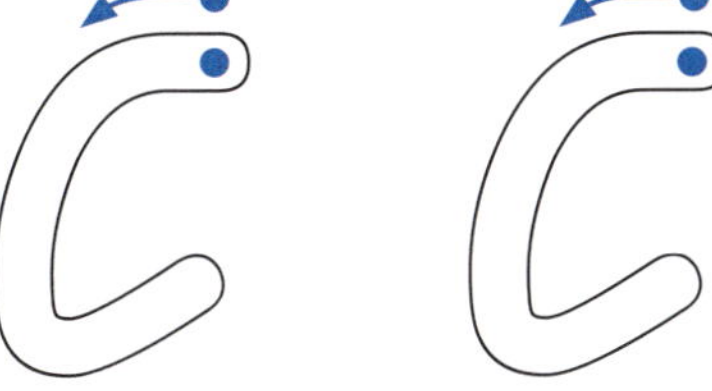
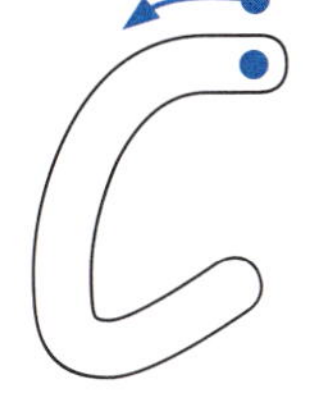

Trace.

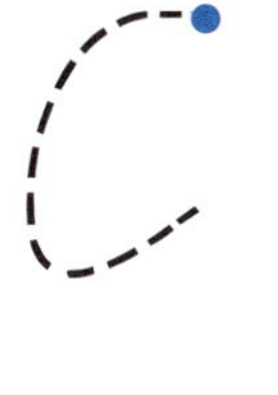

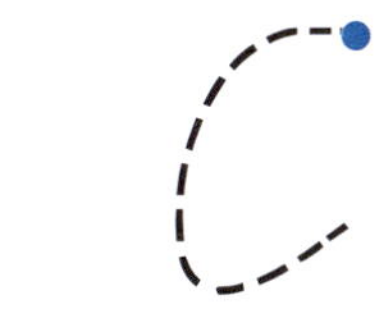
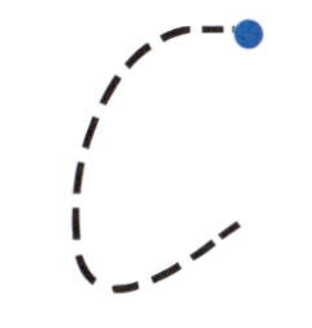
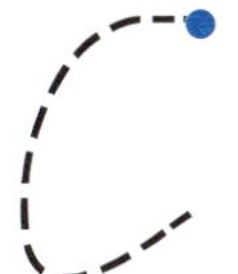

Trace.

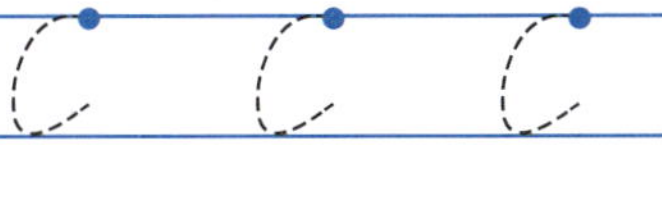
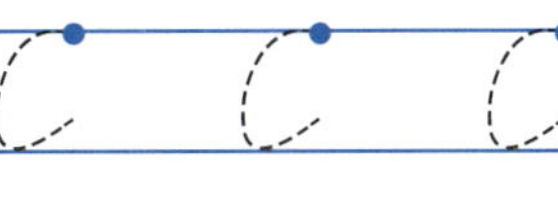
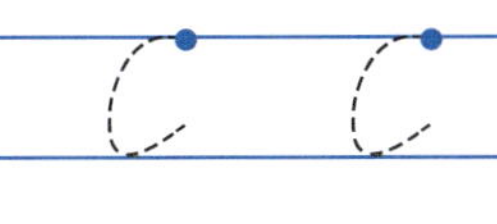
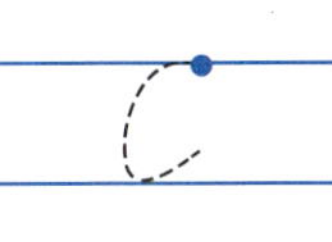
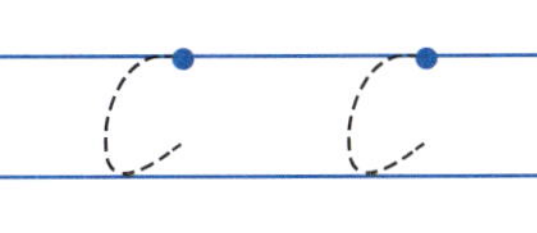
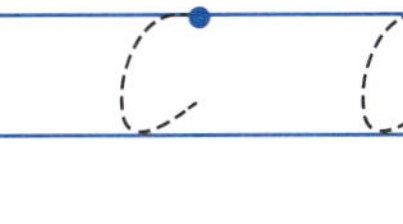

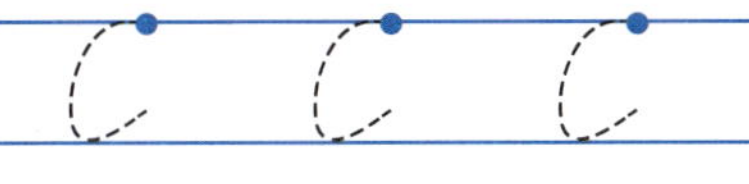
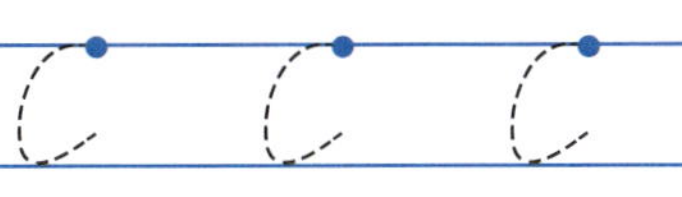
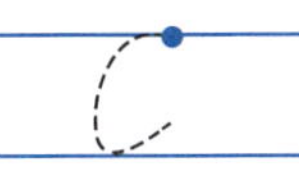
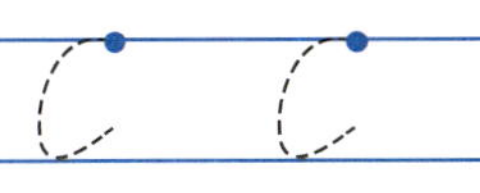
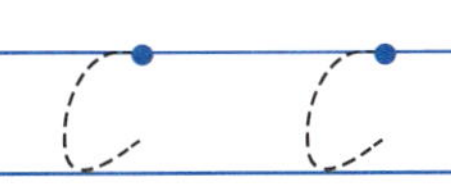

Write.

Patter

Go backwards then curve down, make a quick turn at the bottom. Keep your pencil on the page.

Chant:

frisky frog
f f f

Trace the pattern.

Trace the pattern. Keep your pencil on the page.

Find and write f.

Track.

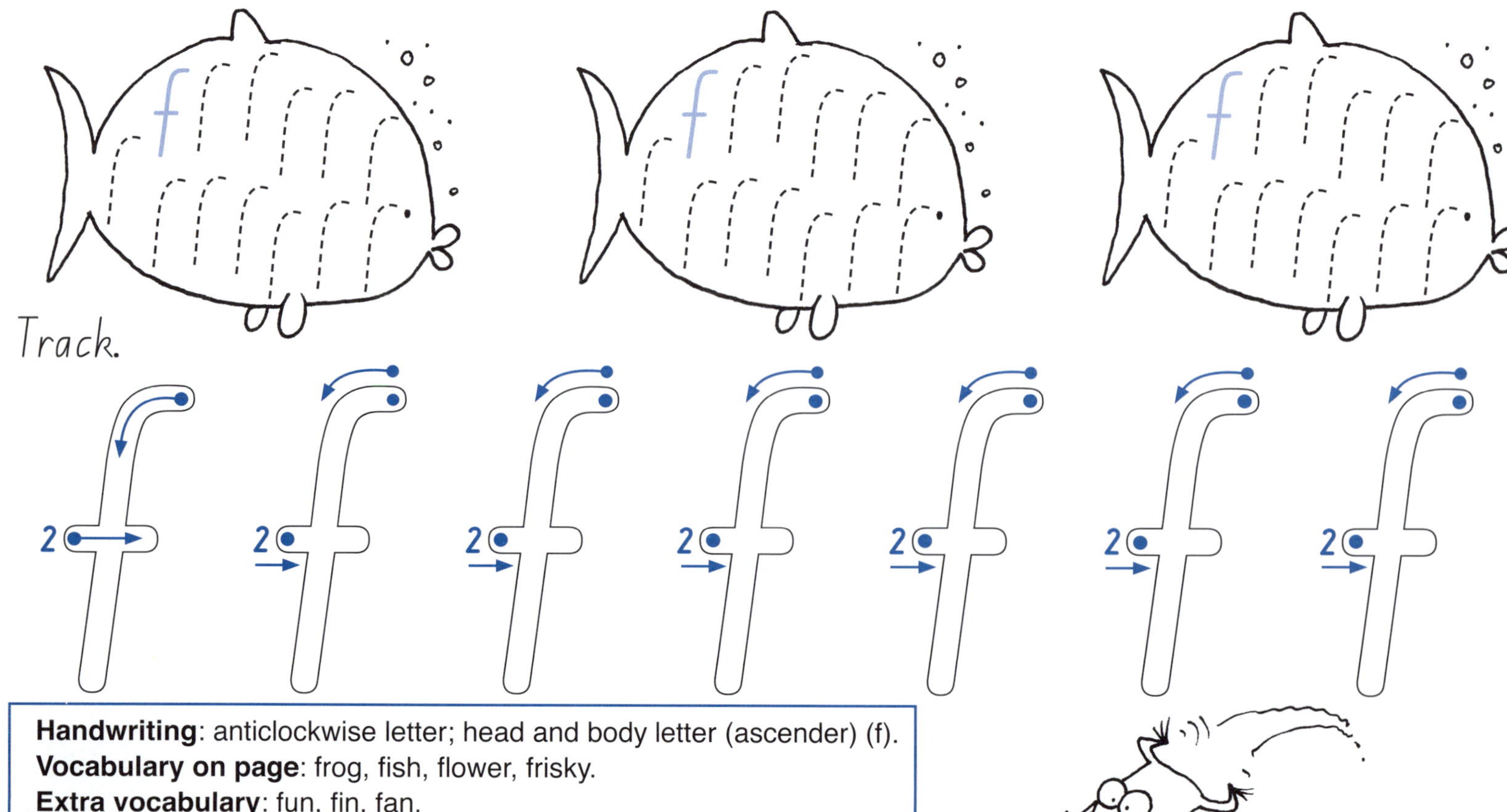

Handwriting: anticlockwise letter; head and body letter (ascender) (f).
Vocabulary on page: frog, fish, flower, frisky.
Extra vocabulary: fun, fin, fan.

f F

Track.

Trace.

Trace.

Write.

Go backwards along the line, curve and slope straight down. Lift your pencil and make a cross.

Chant:

giggly goanna
g g g

Trace the pattern.

Trace the pattern.

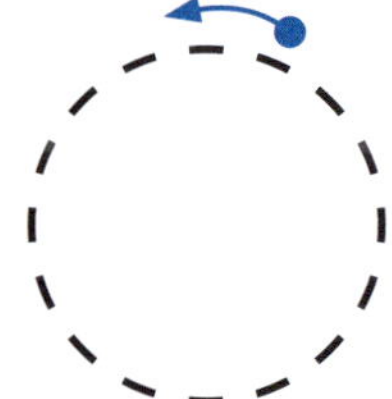   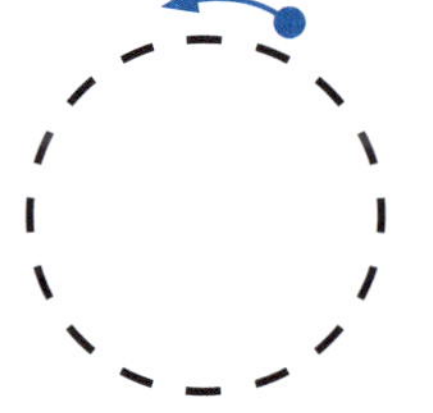 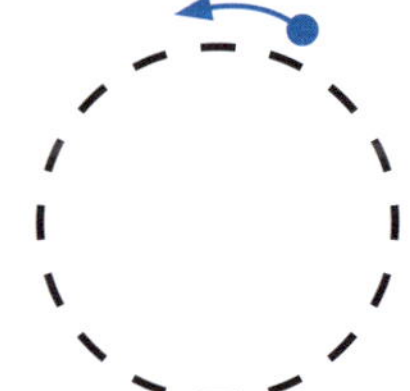 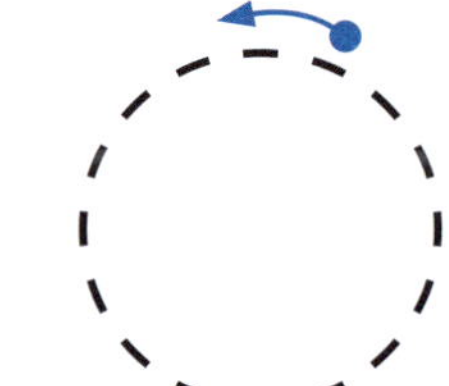

Trace the pattern.

Track.

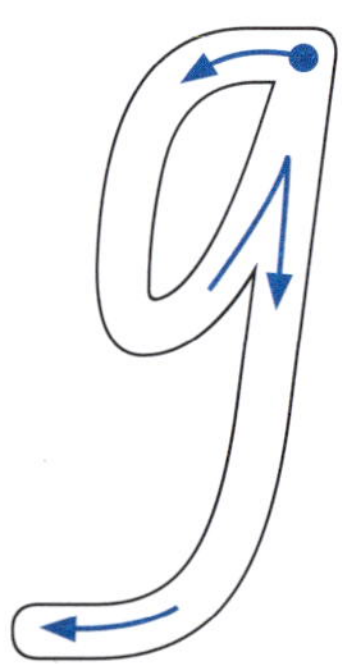 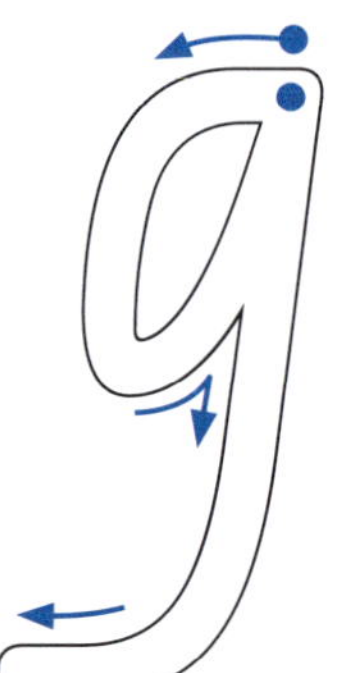  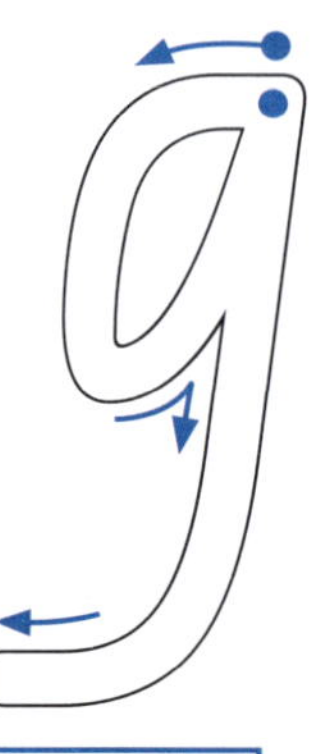 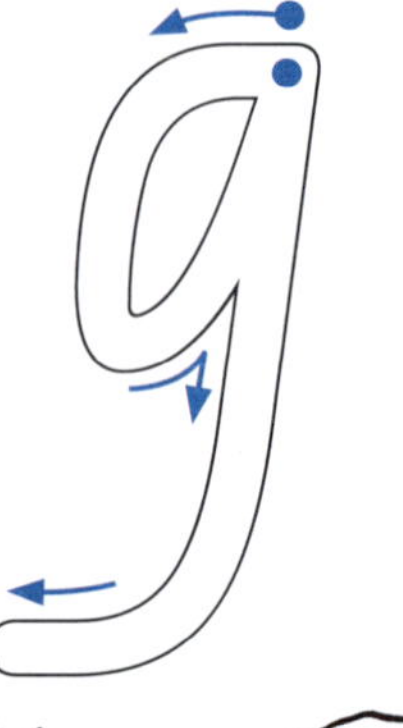 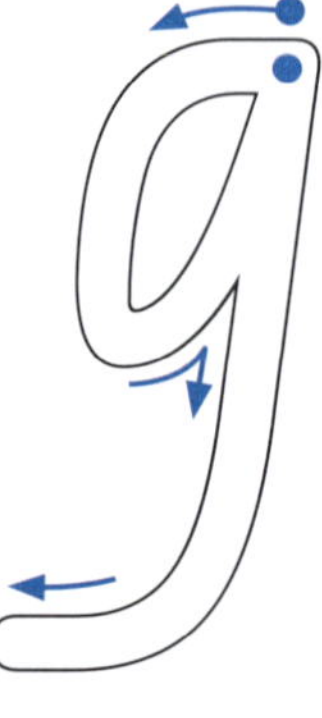

Handwriting: direction change letter; body and tail letter (descender) (g).
Vocabulary on page: giggly, goanna.
Extra vocabulary: get, go, got, pig, dig, dog, hog, jog, egg.

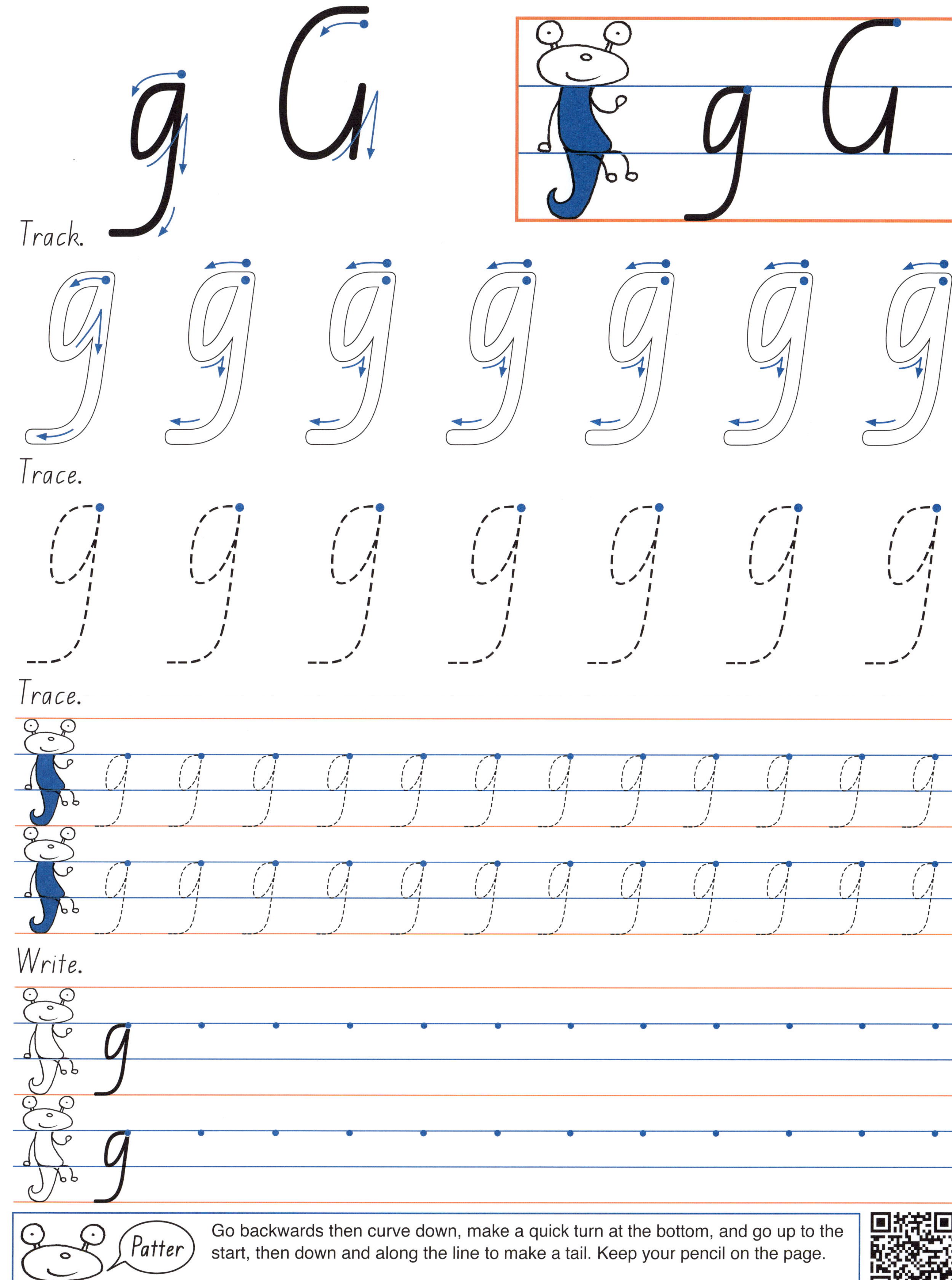

Go backwards then curve down, make a quick turn at the bottom, and go up to the start, then down and along the line to make a tail. Keep your pencil on the page.

Chant:

yellow yak

y y y

Trace the pattern.

Trace the pattern. Keep your pencil on the page.

Trace the pattern. Turn each pattern into a picture.

Track.

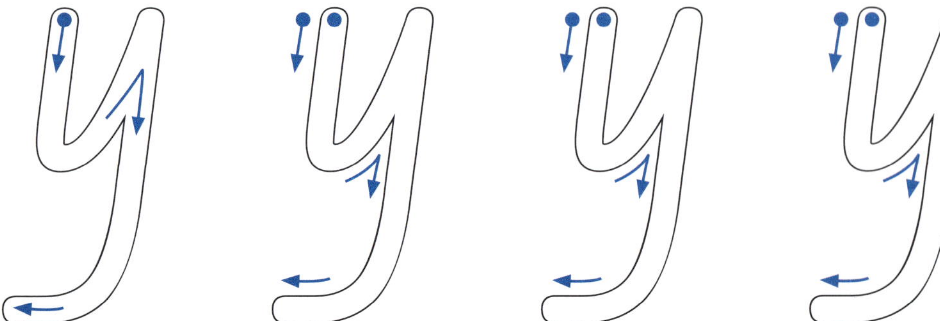

Handwriting: direction change letter; body and tail letter (descender) (y).
Vocabulary on page: yak, yellow.
Extra vocabulary: yell, yes, yo-yo.

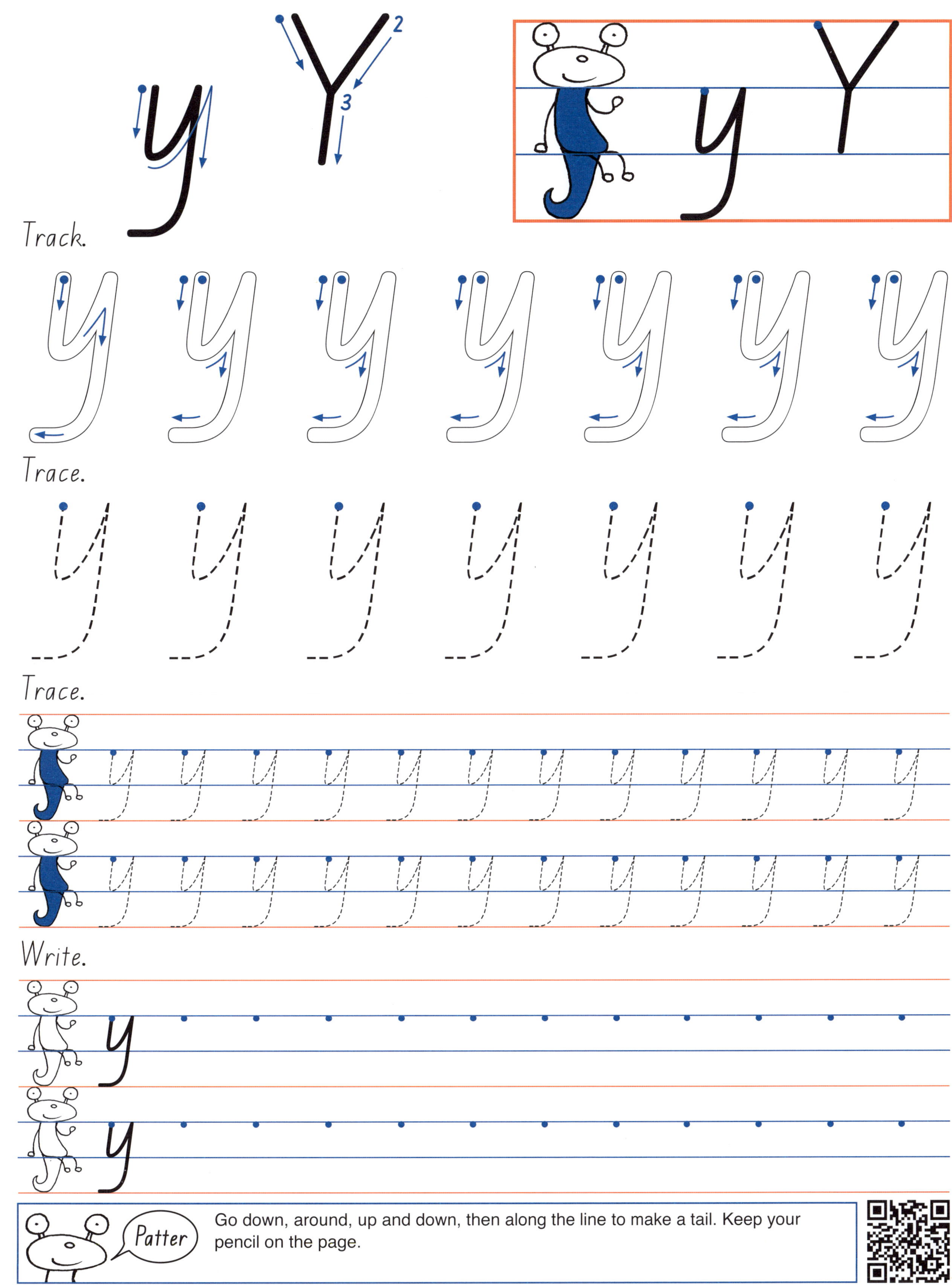

Go down, around, up and down, then along the line to make a tail. Keep your pencil on the page.

Chant:

slippery seal

s s s

Trace the pattern.

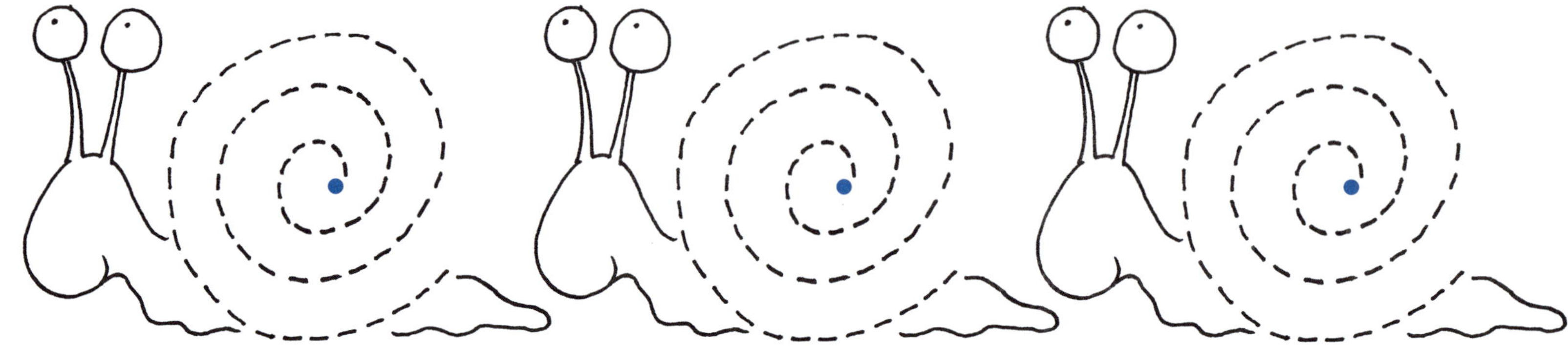

Trace the pattern. Turn the pattern into snakes.

Trace the pattern. Keep your pencil on the page.

Track.

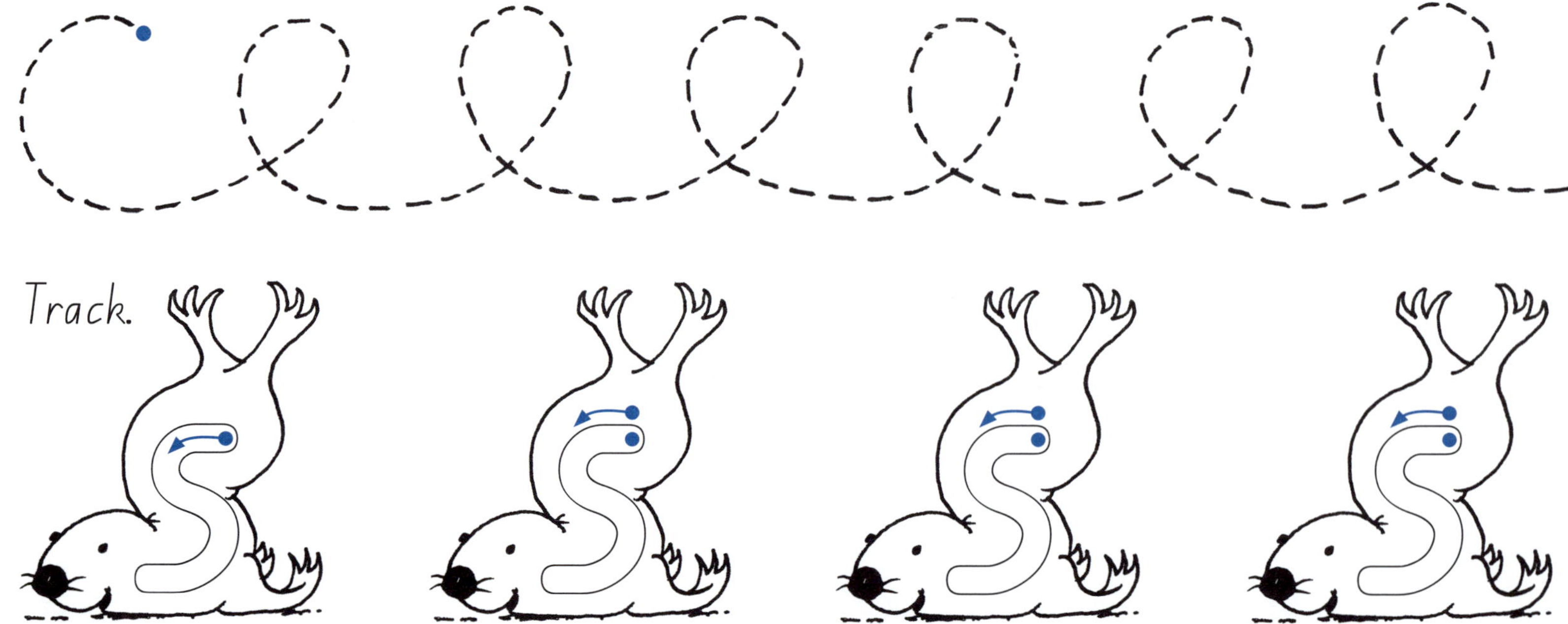

Handwriting: direction change letter; body letter (s).
Vocabulary on page: snake, snail, seal, shear, sheep, slippery, scissors.
Extra vocabulary: so, sit, sat, yes, six, sun, shut, shop, slip.

Go backwards then change direction across the middle, then change direction and finish along the line. Keep your pencil on the page.

one ostrich 1
1
two tigers 2
2
Track.
Track.
Trace.
Trace.
Write.
Write.
Trace the pattern.
Trace the pattern.
Draw 1 thing.
Draw 2 things.

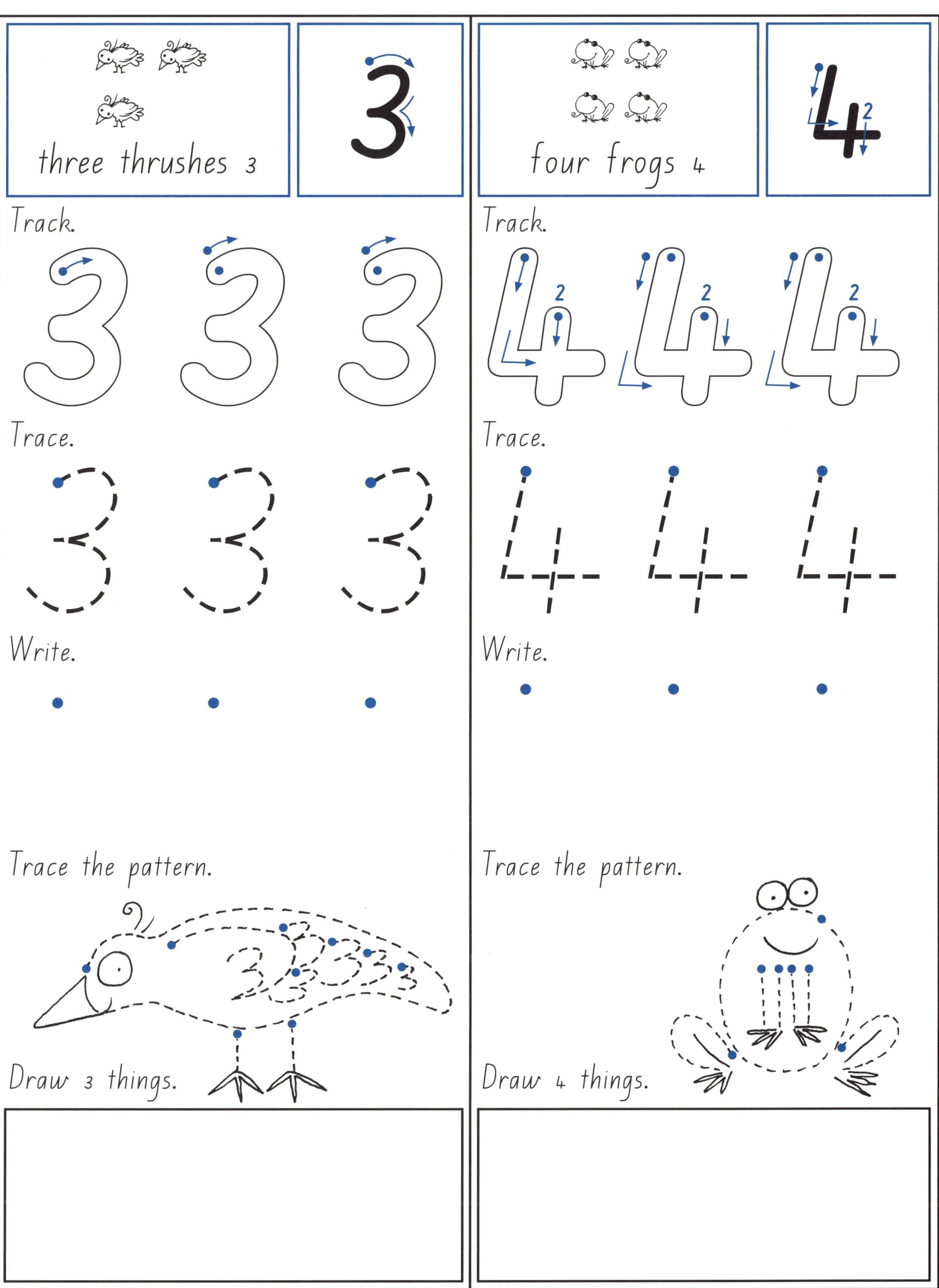
three thrushes 3
3
four frogs 4
4
2
Track.
2
2
2
Track.
Trace.
Trace.
Write.
Write.
Trace the pattern.
Trace the pattern.
Draw 3 things.
Draw 4 things.

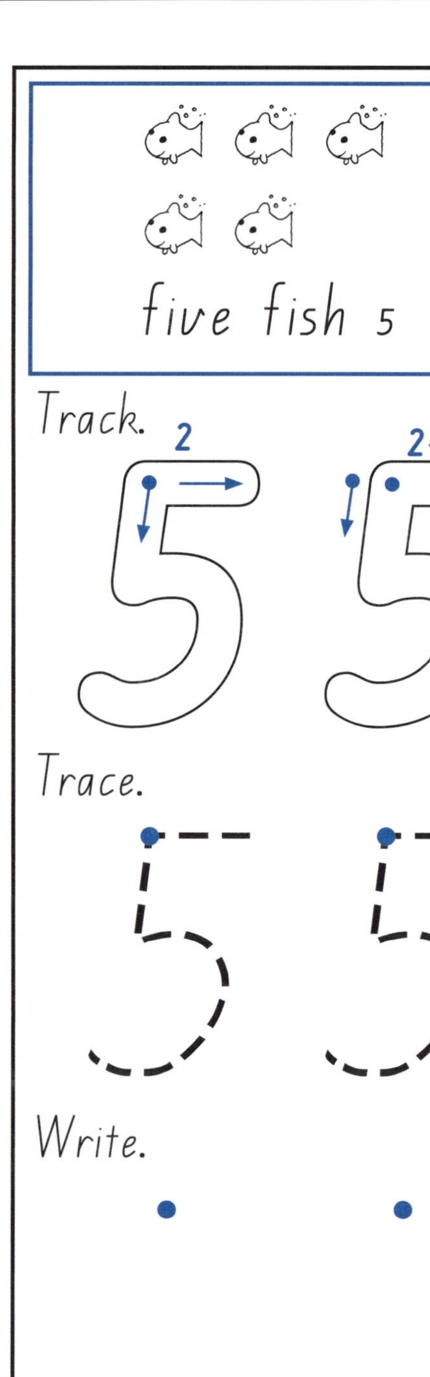

five fish 5

Track.

Trace.

Write.

Trace the pattern.

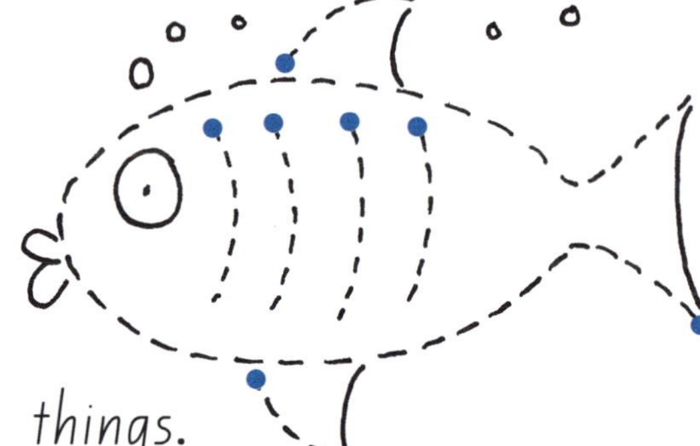

Draw 5 things.

six snails 6

Track.

Trace.

Write.

Trace the pattern.

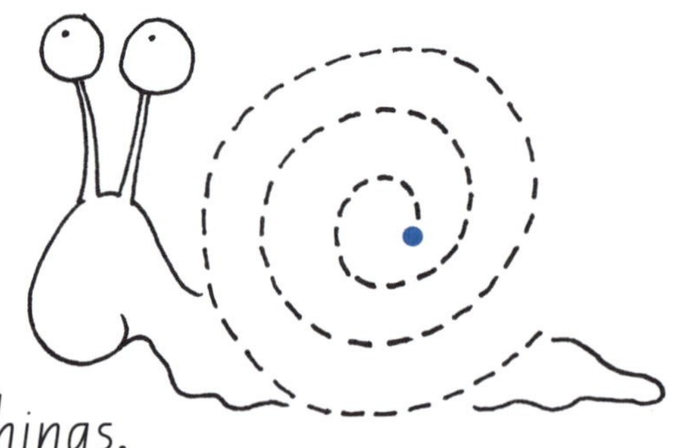

Draw 6 things.

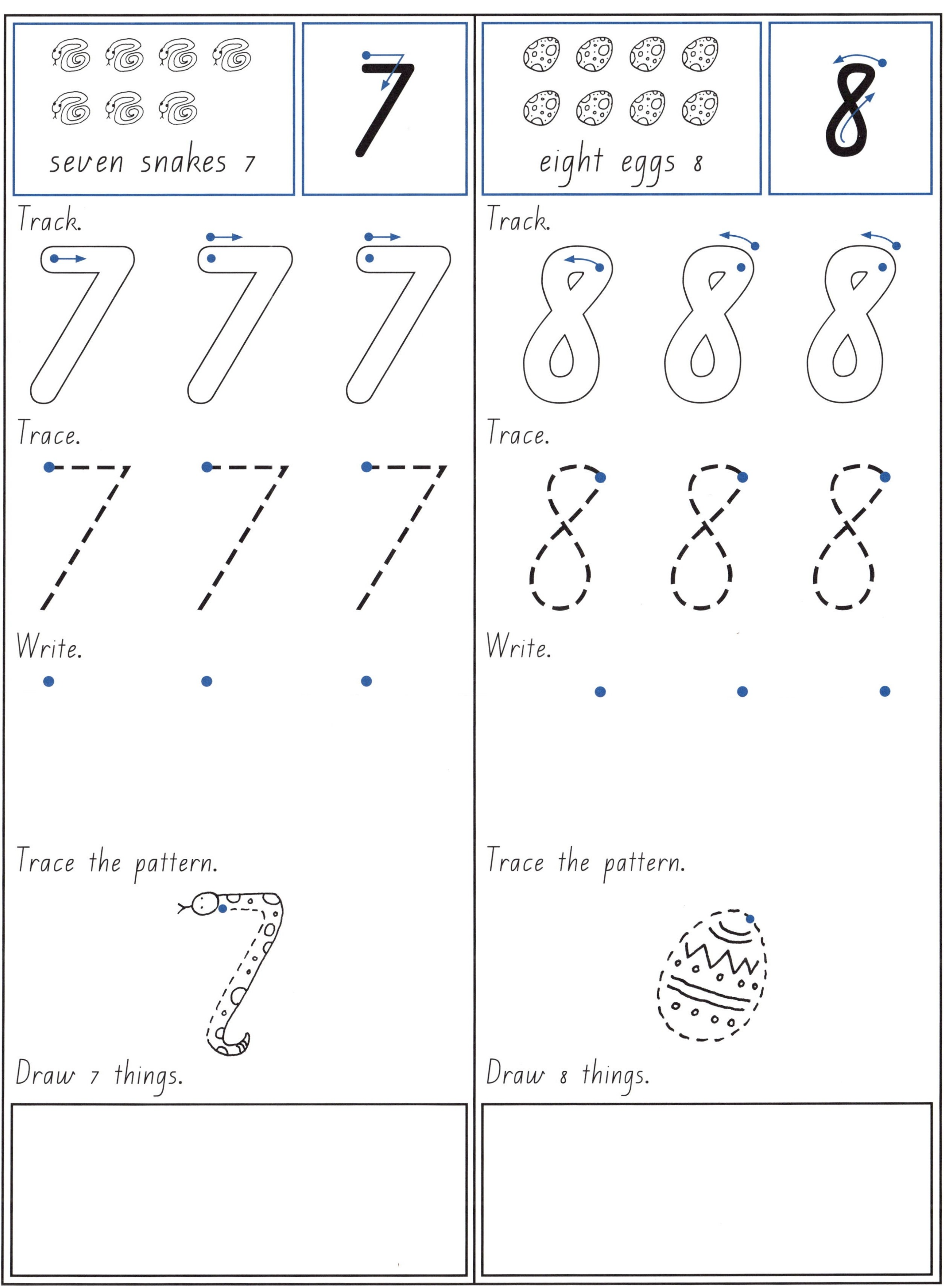
seven snakes 7
7
eight eggs 8
8
Track.
Trace.
Write.
Trace the pattern.
Draw 7 things.
Track.
Trace.
Write.
Trace the pattern.
Draw 8 things.

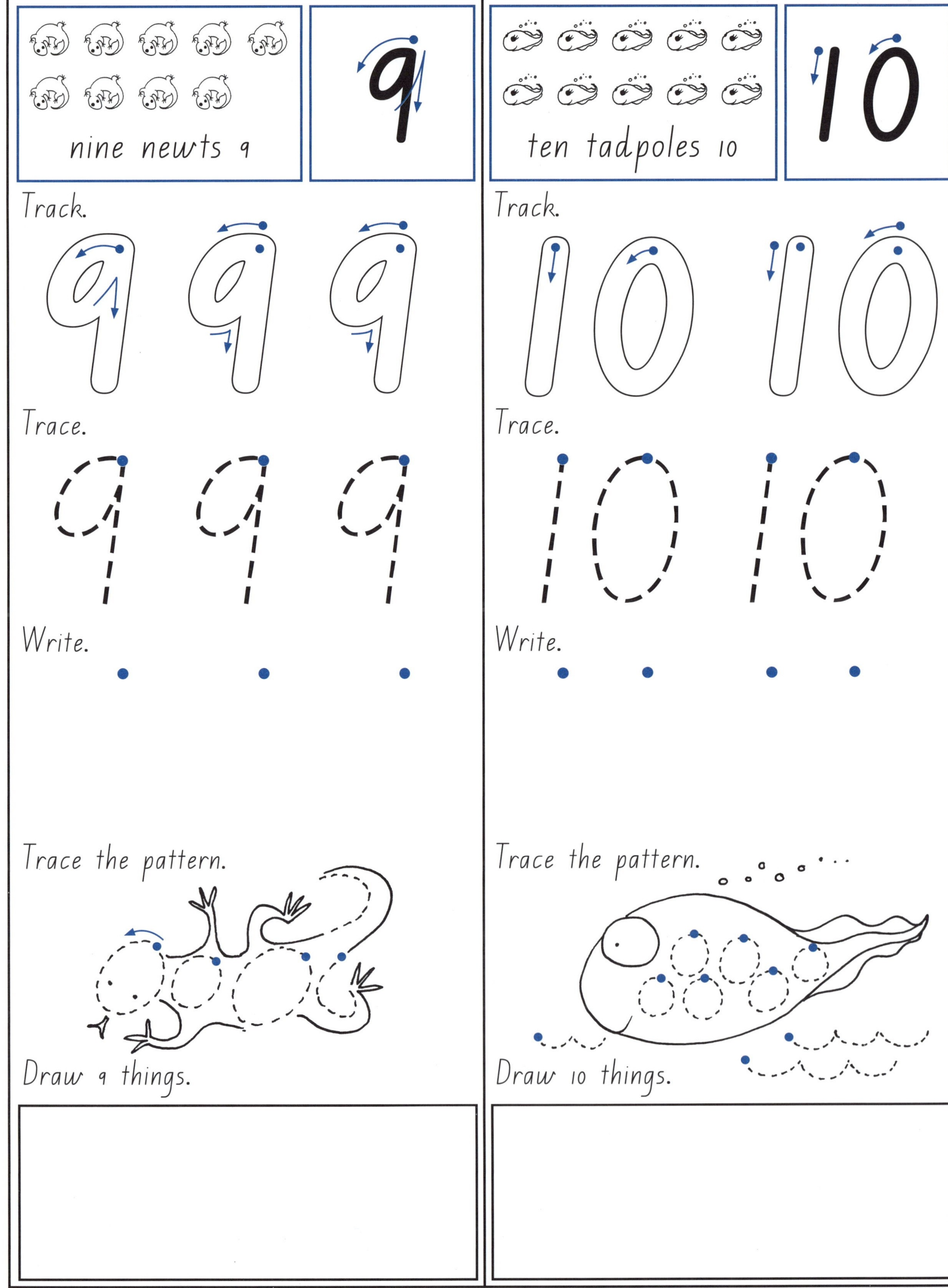
nine newts 9
9
ten tadpoles 10
10
Track.
Trace.
Write.
Trace the pattern.
Draw 9 things.
Track.
Trace.
Write.
Trace the pattern.
Draw 10 things.